STUDYING
THE
TORAH

STUDYING
THE
TORAH

A Guide to
In-Depth Interpretation

Avigdor Bonchek

JASON ARONSON INC.
Northvale, New Jersey
London

First Jason Aronson Inc. softcover edition—1997

This book was set in 12 pt. Garamond by AeroType, Inc.

Library of Congress Cataloging-in-Publication Data

Bonchek, Avigdor.
    Studying the Torah : a guide to in-depth interpretation / by Avigdor Bonchek.
       p. cm.
    Includes index.
    ISBN 1-56821-504-5 (hardcover)
    ISBN 0-7657-9964-2 (softcover)
    1. Bible. O.T. Pentateuch—Criticism, interpretation, etc. I. Title.
BS1225.2.B65   1996
222'.106—dc20

                                    95-38538

Manufactured in the United States of America. Jason Aronson Inc. offers books and cassettes. For information and catalog write to Jason Aronson Inc., 230 Livingston Street, Northvale, New Jersey 07647.

In fond dedication

to

Shulamit,

my devoted wife

and

C. E. Y. M. S. and A.,

our loving children

In memory

of

Zanvel Klein, Ph.D, ע"ה

1937-1991

a lifelong friend

צר לי עליך, אחי, נעמת לי מאוד

(שמואל כ"א : כו)

Contents

Preface

Several years ago, while doing my weekly jogging at the Jerusalem "Y" track, I saw this fellow running some 20–30 meters ahead of me, all decked out in white—white baseball cap, white T-shirt, white shorts, white socks, and white sneakers—a snowy mirage in the dazzling Jerusalem sunshine. As I pulled abreast of him, I saw a tall, sixtyish man, clean shaven and fit-looking. Not missing a step, he turned toward me and said, "You must certainly be reviewing *mishnayot* as you jog!" "Not exactly," I had to admit. He: "I am. I always do." Then, without slowing his pace, he recited the seventeenth chapter of the tractate of *Keilim,* a most obscure corner of the Talmud, and engaged me in a brisk discussion on the purity of vessels; by the tenth lap, I had to call it quits.

The symbolism of that running commentary was not lost on me. So it has been for thousands of years. Today's Jew may jog, the medieval (and recent) European Jew all too often ran for his life, the ancient Jew may have strolled in his vineyard, all the while meditating on his Torah as he "goes on the way, as he lies down, and as he rises up"—a Bible-intoxicated people. This idealized portrait may not be that far from reality.

The religious Jew has always accepted the study of Torah as central to his way of life. More noteworthy, though, is the recent development of the university-educated, worldly, sophisticated, secular reader of today who finds challenge and pleasure in a religious document created three thousand years ago in the sands of Sinai.

As I write this, we are nearing the culmination of the millennium. The period has seen the Bible's unquestioned authority stripped from it. The intellectual crosswinds of history have battered the credentials of the Bible, its historical veracity, its moral relevancy, and its spiritual legitimacy. In spite of all this, we are apt to find the late twentieth-century academic scholar settling down to study the Bible with literary scalpel and magnifying glass in hand. A new respect and fascination is in the air.

Along with the technological progress of the past centuries and the dizzying pace of change in recent decades, man's ideas, beliefs and view of himself have all undergone radical changes. Yet the Bible survives and stands as an immutable and invincible monument rising among the cultural shards of man's history. What is it about The Book that makes it immortal and forever intriguing? The question is best left unanswered. It says more than any conceivable answer could.

For the Jew, the Bible—his Torah—is actually two Torahs. That term encompasses both the *Torah Sh'Bichtav,* the Written Law (Pentateuch, Prophets, and Writings), and the *Torah Sh'B'al Peh,* the Oral Law (the Talmud, Midrash, and Commentaries). These comprise that unique reservoir of religious/cultural heritage from ancient Israel which has been the lifeblood of the Jewish experience.

For myself, I can say that I too have been obsessed with the Torah for many years. I have been particularly fascinated by the text itself, the *Torah Sh'Bichtav*—the Written Law. Its words. Their inexhaustible fertility. No matter how many times I study it and its commentaries, I find new and different insights, nuances, perceptions, and profundities that somehow escaped all previous attempts to understand it.

This book is my attempt to share with others the methods of in-depth interpretation that I have gleaned over the years. The Torah scholar is certainly aware of them, though he may never have articulated them as I have here. Many students and interested laymen, on the other hand, have yet to discover the extent of the Torah's spiritual depth and literary beauty. It is here that I see the contribution of this book. Equipped with these interpretive keys, the study of the Bible becomes an exciting, interactive experience. The Scripture comes alive as the student learns to tease and squeeze from its words a host of unexpected inner meanings.

A word about my terminology: I have used the words Torah, Bible, and Scripture interchangeably. Strictly speaking, the term Torah refers to the Pentateuch (the Five Books of Moses) alone. And, while the overwhelming majority of my examples are drawn from the Pentateuch, the interpretive principles apply to the Jewish Bible literature in general.

Regarding the sources for the many interpretations I make use of throughout the book, the majority of the exegetical examples cited are drawn from the classical Jewish commentators. Several are my own. The reasonableness of these

interpretations is left for the reader to judge. The rule I
follow (as did the classical Jewish commentators) is that
interpretations must stand on their own merit. A home-
grown insight is as good as, better than, or worse than one
from a venerated commentator, depending on how well it
passes the test of rational critique.

I have called these methods Keys to Interpretation. I
have chosen the word *keys* because the techniques are
meant to unlock the treasures of beauty and power that
are contained within the words of the Bible. Two clarifica-
tions are in order. First, these are not my keys; I did not
develop them. They are the interpretative tools used by
the rabbinic biblical scholars and can be found in the vast
exegetical literature which was produced from the elev-
enth through the nineteenth centuries. And second, the
keys discussed herein do not exhaust the types of interpretative tools available. Some I have intentionally left
out; others I have yet to learn.

My use of the word *keys* is meant to be a double en-
tendre, hinting also at musical keys. As are musical keys,
these analytical keys can be artfully used, combined in an
infinite variety of ways to give expression to the music of
the text. The latent meanings, the music resonating from
its words, have been there all along. Our task is to get
these words to speak to us again in all their profundity
and, in this way, to let the Scripture sing!

Acknowledgments

This book would never have been written were it not for the inspiration and encouragement of two people. They are my beloved wife, Shulamit, and Professor Nechama Leibowitz, a close friend and admired teacher.

Professor Leibowitz's skillful analysis of the Torah and its commentaries has opened my eyes to the inspiring challenge of *P'shat* interpretation. Her books, lectures, and our many personal discussions have made me acutely aware that when it comes to the Written Law, there is more mystery in the visible than in the invisible. Thanks to her, I have learned a simple, enlightening lesson: Take the Torah text seriously. It is this lesson that stands behind every example in this book. Those familiar with her works will recognize those parts of this book that owe their source directly to her. I am particularly indebted to her for the material in chapter 7. However, this book was written without her knowledge (though we discussed it after I had completed it), so she should certainly not be held accountable for any weakness in its content or style.

Energy of a different kind was provided by my wife, Shulamit. Her unwavering encouragement kept me going the many months during which time this book was written and rewritten. Her natural eye for style and spelling has given the book a necessary added touch. Most certainly, I am indebted to her for much more than just her help in this endeavor. I have been very fortunate to have her as my *"ezer k'negdo."* No tribute is more fitting than Rabbi Akiva's classic praise of his wife to his students: *"sheli v'shelachem, shelah!"*

What I have gained and what the reader may gain from this work are in the greatest part due to her.

I also want to thank my children, Chanoch, Elisheva, Yehoshua, Michal, Shira, and Avi, who are my joint authors. Unbeknownst to them, they had an active part in the creation of this book. Our *Shabbat* table discussions of the weekly *Parsha* provoked many ideas as we grappled with difficulties in the Torah. Some of their original insights have been incorporated into this book and can be found among the many interpretive examples.

Others too have been instrumental in moving this book from personal preoccupation to publishable print. My friend, Chaim Billet, saw the manuscript in its very raw state and nevertheless thought it good enough to show to Arthur Kurzweil at Jason Aronson. Chaim's faith, clairvoyance, and successful matchmaking were my good fortune. Mr. Kurzweil's unstinting optimism and gracious support have fortified me throughout the publishing process.

Several friends, experienced in the publishing world, Dr. Shmuel Himmelstein, Mrs. Wendy Dickstein, and Rabbi Dodi Landesman were kind enough to read the manuscript and offer me their professional advice. And to my *chavrusa*, Yaakov Berman, a special debt of gratitude for his untiring kindness in offering me his advice and use of all his modern paraphernalia—P.C., printer, fax, and his accomplished word processing skills.

Traditional Torah commentators signed off their manuscripts with the following notation. I can do no better.

"Finished and completed. Praise and gratitude to the Creator."

Their commentaries provide additional dimensions to our understanding; these Rabbis and their methods provide depth to interpretation. I use the word ''depth'' here not as a mantra to invoke uncritical adoration or to create the impression of mystery. Depth-in-interpretation is not something to be accepted without reason. It means, quite simply, that the Torah-text, which is apparent to all, accessible to all, can be plumbed to yield layer after layer of textual meaning. The coordinates of interpretation, the validity of interpretation, always remain within the text itself and, thus, are available for all to evaluate.

Keys to Interpretation

While interpretation always involves differences of opinion, there are, nevertheless, certain ground rules of interpretation which are agreed upon. The most basic rule is that Plain Sense interpretation must plainly make sense! It must strive to be true to the text. The text is our point of departure, our guideline as we search for meaning in the Torah, and ultimately, our end point as we return to the text with a deeper understanding of it.

The classical Torah commentators have never spelled out the rules which guided them in their interpretive work. In fact, there are no rules per se which exist as hard and fast entities. But, notwithstanding all the differences that exist between the many commentators, their overall approach to the interpretation of the Plain Sense of the Torah revolves around a tacit code of methodological coherence.

In the chapters that follow, I delineate some of the Keys to Interpretation that I believe are essential for acquiring a deeper understanding of the Torah. These Keys, it must be understood, are guidelines which I have inferred from the kinds of questions commentators ask and from the way they go about answering them. To my knowledge, this is the first attempt to abstract, specify, and categorize various keys to classical Torah interpretation. Yet I have no illusions about the completeness of this endeavor. There are undoubtedly important keys that I have missed (and some that I have intentionally left out). I am confident, however, that what I have presented here can serve the student of Torah well. It affords him an opportunity to gain a deep and authentic appreciation of the Torah's beauty and profundity. Hopefully, it will enable him also to discover new insights into the Torah.

What Is In-Depth Interpretation?

By In-Depth Interpretation of the Torah, we mean interpretation that is both firmly based on the written text yet, at the same time, that goes beyond its literal meaning. In-Depth Interpretation of *P'shat* infuses the flat text with resonance and power. The simple biblical story is transformed into a universally relevant moral lesson, a terse biblical conversation becomes a study in skillful psychological nuancing, and a catalogue of legal edicts opens up a window into the human soul.

What exactly do we mean by In-Depth Interpretation? The mere attribution of ''depth'' to a statement is often meant to give it an aura of indisputable authority and esoteric knowledge. This is not our intent. We do not mean ''depth'' in the sense of mystical interpretations or even those of the midrashic kind. These interpretations have different sources in the human psyche and strike different chords in the human mind. They have their own rules of interpretation, which are different from those of *P'shat* and are much more difficult to pin down. Because of the arcane nature of these latter interpretations, students unfamiliar with them may be suspicious of them, feeling that they exploit the text in ways that appear both undisciplined and arbitrary.

Popularized psychological interpretations of human behavior have added to our suspiciousness of "deep" interpretations. I remember about twenty years ago when I told a psychologist friend that I couldn't swim and that I couldn't float on my back for fear of getting water in my eyes, nose, and mouth. He recommended psychoanalysis. I said that I thought swimming lessons were more appropriate (and less expensive). He explained that my fear was of a much deeper nature. I was, first of all, afraid of letting go, fear of swimming being just a convenient symptom of this problem. But more profound was my unconscious conflict between wanting to return to the "oceanic feeling" of being in the womb (and the amniotic fluids) on one hand and my fear of entrapment in a Mrs. Portnoy-type symbiosis on the other. This, I was given to understand, was the deeper meaning of my unremarkable fear.

Such prepackaged "depth" insights make most of us uncomfortable. It almost seems that the further an interpretation distances itself from common sense, the "deeper" it is considered to be.

So, too, with pseudo-deep interpretations of the Torah. The untrained student may think that the further we are taken from a reasonable sense of the text, the more "deeply" we have plumbed its mysteries. If that were, in fact, the case, then depth-interpretation would require

constant suspension of our rational judgment. For many,
that is an unreasonable price to pay for understanding the
Torah. I believe that it is not only unreasonable but also
unnecessary. The Scriptures are truly profound, my ap-
probation not being necessary on that account. What I
hope to show in this book is that this depth is not discovered by arbitrary free-association or undisciplined flights
of fancy. Rules and guidelines exist which can help us
objectify the parameters of depth-interpretation. Familiarity with these rules makes the discovery of the truly
deep meanings in the Torah that much more gratifying,
intellectually and spiritually.

What the Text Says . . . How It Says It

We can point out two fundamental parameters of interpretation which will clarify our meaning of depth interpretation and will orient the student toward the deeper
layers of Scriptural meaning.

"What" the Text Says

The starting point for all interpretation is to know *what*
the text says. This is obvious. Yet knowing what any word
or sentence means is not always that obvious. We must
work from the original Hebrew. All translations are necessarily interpretations and all interpretations are open to
dispute. This puts the student who works from an English
text at a distinct disadvantage. This is not to say that
depth-interpretation can never be done from a translation; only that, when working from a translation, one
must be more careful. In this book, when the original
Hebrew differs from accepted translations, I will point

this out. As we will see, these differences are sometimes very significant.

But even when using the Hebrew text, the *what* is not always clear. The commentators frequently suggest different interpretations of the same word and phrase. At times, the differences are important.

In the story of the ten plagues, we read: "And the engravers (magicians) did so with their secret arts to bring out (*L'Hotzie*) gnats, but they could not . . ." (Exodus 8:14). Now the word *L'Hotzie* can mean "to bring out" ("to cause more gnats to come out"). It can also mean "to take out" ("to remove them"). These are not only different meanings, they are opposite meanings. In the first case, the engravers were competing with Moses to bring out even more gnats. While this would increase the suffering of the Egyptians, it would nevertheless undermine the uniqueness of Moses' plague. The second interpretation of *L'Hotzie* ("to remove") means simply that the engravers tried to undo Moses' plague, to bring relief to the people. These very different interpretations are offered respectively by Rashi and the Malbim. Each can find support for his view in the text.

In sum, the first step in understanding the text is to understand *what* is said. In the example above, the *what* was not clear. Many times, however, the *what* is abundantly clear, yet the reader glosses over it without serious reflection. This casual approach to the text deprives him of the opportunity of seeing beneath the surface. My lengthy In-Depth Interpretation of the Ten Plagues (chapter 11) is an example of how paying very close attention to the *what,* to every nuance in the text, can expose an unexpected perspective of the many levels of meaning contained within the story. It also illustrates how an In-

Depth Interpretation takes us beyond the text into the realm of sophisticated biblical theology, all of this accomplished with our interpretive coordinates firmly anchored in the text, while never abandoning our commitment to the exclusive authority of the text.

How It Is Said

If the *what* of the text is interpretation's most fundamental aspect, the *how it is said* is interpretation's most fascinating aspect.

The bulk of this book, most of my Keys to Interpretation, is based on *how* the Torah tells us *what* it wants us to hear. This is where the Torah's subtlety of expression, cadence in communication, and poetry in prose maximizes its avenues of meaning. This is where the depth is found in Torah interpretation.

To illustrate, let us look at several sentences in the story of the rape of Dinah:

And Dinah, the daughter of Leah, whom she bare unto Jacob, went out to see among the daughters of the land. And when Shechem, the son of Hamor the Hivite, prince of the country, saw her, he took her, and lay with her, and afflicted her. And his soul clave unto Dinah, the daughter of Jacob, and he loved the damsel and spake lovingly to the damsel. And Shechem spake unto his father Hamor, saying, Take me this young girl to wife. (Genesis 34:1–4)

What has been said here? That Dinah went out and was raped by Shechem, that he wants her for his wife and asks his father to arrange the matter. But *how* has it been said?

Look at how variously Dinah is referred to in these few sentences:

> Dinah, daughter of Leah (when she went out) (Genesis 34:1);
>
> her, her, her, her (when raped and used as a sex object) (Genesis 34:2).
>
> Dinah, daughter of Jacob (desired to marry her) (Genesis 34:3);
>
> damsel, damsel (when speaking to her) (Genesis 34:3);
>
> young girl (when speaking to father about her) (Genesis 34:4).

This intentional interchanging of adjectives, nouns, pronouns, and proper nouns has the inescapable effect of taking us into the heads of the individual players in this drama. Dinah acted like her mother (daughter of Leah) who walked about freely in search of her sexual partner (see Rashi). Shechem rapes her and relates to her as an impersonal object, "her" (in Hebrew: *Otah,* which means both "her" and "it"). This object then is transformed into a princess (daughter of Jacob) when he thinks of marriage to her. When romancing her, he uses the universal masculine ploy of showing her great admiration and respect ("damsel"), in spite of his obvious disdain (having raped and afflicted her); and to his father, he calls her a mere child!

This is but one of endless examples of the ways in which the Torah sculpts the text to convey meaning beyond the *what* of the story. The Torah is replete with a host of

similar examples of word play, repetition, word association, nimble verbal nuances, and the like. Understanding
these instances of the *how* of biblical communication
ultimately enriches us with a fuller appreciation for the
depth of Torah interpretation.

Being familiar with the rules of interpretation is essential to gaining an in-depth understanding of the Torah. Yet
knowing the rules does not guarantee us correct understanding. Interpretation is a complex art. We can misin-
terpret and, as a consequence, we can misunderstand.
The classic commentaries frequently vie with each over
their view of the correct interpretation of a particular
passage or chapter, each having his reasons for preferring
his particular interpretation.

Validity in Interpretation

How is one to decide which interpretation leads to the
best understanding of the text? A cautious view would
be that the most we can strive for is relative validation of
any interpretation, since we have no way of being abso-
lutely certain what the Torah's true intent was. Certainly
some interpretations sound better than others. But are
there rules which we can apply to guide us in our search?
Have we any means of evaluating the validity of different
interpretations?

We must hedge our answer on this. On the one hand, no
one has discovered a fool-proof method of arriving at
correct interpretation. On the other, there can be agree-
ment about an incorrect interpretation when it is glaringly
wrong. It is, rather, the vast middle ground of interpretations that confuses us. Here the classic commentators show

us their skill and wisdom in pointing out the strengths and weaknesses of possible interpretative options.

In light of this, interpretations should be seen as relatively valid, that is, as better or worse than other possible interpretations. I would suggest two general rules for evaluating the relative validity of alternative interpretations. These rules can, of course, also be used by the student to discover new interpretations in the text.

Text-in-Context

We intuitively interpret on the basis of the *text-in-context.* That is, the meaning of any text or communication is dependent on the context within which it is imbedded. The same words convey different meanings when they exist in different contextual settings. Likewise, different words may convey similar meanings when they exist in similar contexts.

What this means is that every part of a passage derives its meaning from its surrounding context. Simple enough and obvious, isn't it? If you think so, then let's test your wits.

We'll look at a short biblical passage and see if you can answer a simple question. The passage is from Genesis, chapter 42. I'll give you some background, then we'll see the passage, then I'll pop the question.

The brothers of Joseph go down to Egypt to buy food for their famine-stricken families. Joseph, the Viceroy of Egypt, recognizes them, while they don't recognize him. He accuses them of spying. Joseph demands that they bring their youngest brother to him.

Bring your youngest brother to me, so your words be verified, and you shall not die. And they did so. And

they said one to another, We are verily guilty concerning our brother, in that we saw the distress of his
soul, when he implored us, and we would not hear.
Therefore is this distress come upon us. And Reuben
answered them, saying, Said I not to you as follows:
Do not sin against the child; and you would not hear?
Therefore, behold, also his blood is required. And
they knew not that Joseph understood them; for the
interpreter was between them. And he turned away
from them, and wept; and he returned to them, and
he spoke to them, and he took from them Simeon and
bound him before their eyes. (Genesis 42:20)

The need to understand is the beginning of interpretation. What we need to understand here, among other
things, is why Joseph picked Simeon, of all the brothers,
to hold as ransom? Can you derive an answer from the
passage? You can't brush off the question with a wave of
the hand and say that this was an arbitrary choice. If that
were the case, then the Torah would not have named
Simeon by name. For example, earlier it says, anony-
mously, "And they said one to another," because the
identity of those speaking is not essential to understanding the passage. But here Simeon is mentioned by name,
implying that this choice had a particular meaning.

Another problem in the text is the non sequitur "And
they didn't know that Joseph understood them." What
purpose do these words serve in the story?

Keep in mind the principle of Text-in-Context and see if
you can come up with an interpretation.

Time's up!

Now look at those words again, "And they didn't know
that Joseph understood. . . ." I suggest that they provide

the "context" which makes it possible for us to understand why Simeon was chosen. "And Reuben answered . . .
'Said I not to you . . . Do not sin against the child, and
you would not hear?'" We are told that Reuben, the
firstborn, and natural leader of the family, had tried to
save Joseph, something that we, the readers, already knew
but something that Joseph certainly did not know all the
years of his exile in Egypt. As he thought about
his abduction, he likely assumed that, had his oldest
brother, Reuben, tried to save him, he would have been
saved. All those years he had probably harbored a strong
resentment toward Reuben for not having saved him.
Now Joseph heard for the first time ("and they knew
not that Joseph understood them . . .") that Reuben had
indeed tried to save him. Once Joseph heard this, he
realized that responsibility for selling him into slavery
now fell upon the next oldest brother, Simeon! "And he
took from them Simeon." I like this explanation. I think
it effortlessly answers our questions. It was offered by
Abraham Ibn Ezra (1089–1164).

The Torah uses words sparingly. Phrases are chosen
with a premeditated conception and a fine-tuned sensitivity to what the reader needs to hear in order to understand its message. At the same time, the Torah is quite
subtle in its method of conveying its message. A sharp eye
and sensitive ear are necessary to mine its meaning.

But even more important than this reading skill is one's
basic attitude toward the Torah-text. Essential to produc-
tive and creative In-Depth Interpretation of the Torah is a
deep-seated respect for the significance of every word
and every nuance in the text. The attitude that nothing in
the text is for naught is the springboard which impels us
in our search for meaning in the Torah. This attitude

hardens into firm conviction the more one successfully
probes the depths of Torah interpretation.

In summary, we can say that the closer an interpretation
is to the surrounding context, the more it satisfies our
expectations of a valid interpretation.

The Law of Parsimony in Interpretation

Rashi (1040–1105) deals with the same question as to why
Simeon was chosen by Joseph. He makes the following
comment: "It was Joseph's intention to separate him from
Levi, lest the two of them conspire to kill him." Rashi
bases this interpretation on the presupposition that Simeon and Levi are "blood" brothers. They conspired together to wipe out the city of Shechem to save their sister
Dinah and avenge her honor. They are thus capable of
killing this heathen to save Benjamin.

This explanation is based on information we have from
the text in another episode about the brothers (the slaugh-
ter of Shechem) and thus has some connection to the
larger context of meaning related to the brothers' lives.

Yet Ibn Ezra's interpretation impresses us as offering a
better fit with the whole passage. Why so?

In answering that question, we arrive at another principle of interpretation. Interpretation strives for simplicity as it aims for understanding. There are preferences
in interpretation. The simple interpretation is preferred
over the complex; the comprehensive explanation is preferred over the circumscribed. An interpretation that
resolves several difficulties in the text in one fell swoop
is not only more elegant, it also has the ring of truth. This
is Parsimony in Interpretation. Simplicity and compre-
hensiveness are basic characteristics of sound interpreta-

tion. It is our second rule for arriving at veracity in interpretation.

When we compare the two interpretations above, that of Ibn Ezra and that of Rashi, we see that Ibn Ezra's interpretation of why Simeon was chosen resolves several difficulties in the passage. It explains not only why Simeon was chosen but also why Reuben's statement is quoted, and why we are told that Joseph understood the brothers' remarks. His explanation shows how everything fits into place and how the passage is a cohesive unit. Rashi's explanation gives the reason why Simeon was chosen, but doesn't help us understand more than that.

Ibn Ezra's interpretation is both simpler and more comprehensive than Rashi's. It is more parsimonious. It would seem to offer a better fit to the whole section.

These two primary rules—Text-in-Context and Parsimony in Interpretation—could be considered the meta-rules of Torah interpretation. More focused rules of interpretation, which I call Keys to Understanding, will be elucidated in the following chapters, and form the main body of this book.

Torah: Divine Revelation or Cultural Relic

The Torah is first and foremost a religious book. It is for this reason that any discussion about it is bound to stir emotions, both positive and negative. The religiously committed see it as the revealed word of God, the secular see it as a surprisingly well-preserved document, a relic from Israel's ancient past. The former relate to it as infallible, eternally valid, and Divine; the latter as, at times, inspiring, at times, primitive, an all-too-human and inevitably time-bound record.

For the post-Spinoza enlightened mind to demand that the Torah always make sense, literarily, philosophically, and psychologically, seems a quaint and blushingly naive pursuit. More palatable to those who view faith as a hindrance to intellectual honesty is the uncritical acceptance of the highly problematic Documentary Hypothesis, which has the imprimatur of science. Such an attitude blocks a serious approach to the Torah-text. Why look within the Torah itself for solutions to textual difficulties when they can be assumed to be the result of redactional inaccuracies? Grammatical irregularities, contradictions, and inconsistencies are to be expected in a work that is a patchwork of converging documentary fragments produced in man's primitive past. The unfortunate upshot of this stance is that, for many students, a serious in-depth inquiry into the Torah's meaning is squelched and the richness of its meaning is forever lost to them.

The man of faith runs into a different kind of problem. The committed believer may transfer his unquestioning faith in the Divine origin of the Bible to unquestioning acceptance of a superficial reading of it, whether it makes sense to him or not. Recognizing difficulties in the Torah-text, yet accepting them as being beyond his ability to comprehend, may be considered, by him, to be a sign of his faith. Thus, perceived difficulties in the Scriptures may be repressed, lest pursuing them be seen as a lack of faith. In this way, unflinching inquisitiveness into the Torah may be stifled.

Certainly a man of deeply grounded faith sees matters otherwise. Unfettered questioning is the best expression of one's faith in the ultimate sensibility and wisdom of the Torah.

The Sages put it this way:

> ". . . all the words of this Torah. For it is no empty matter to you . . ." (Deuteronomy 32:47).
>
> Said Rav Mana, "For it is no empty matter *to you,* and if it is empty, to you (alone) is it so. And why is this? Because you haven't struggled with the Torah."

My thesis here is that the Bible's religious profundity, ethical sensitivity, psychological insightfulness, aesthetic beauty and subtlety of expression are available for all to discover and appreciate, regardless of one's religious commitment. The only prerequisites in this exciting and inspiring pursuit are one's respect for the Torah as a sophisticated religious record and an open inquisitive mind. The rest, as Hillel the Elder said, is interpretation. . . . Go and learn!

2

Reading the Torah-Text for Deeper Understanding

If I have given the impression that Torah interpretation is a unidimensional endeavor, then I have unfairly oversimplified matters. Interpretation is a many-splendored thing. Interpretation has many different faces and Torah commentators wear many different hats.

The talmudic Sages taught that every passage of the Torah has seventy facets, perhaps a metaphorical number meant to reflect the seventy scholars of the *Sanhedrin,* whose job it was to interpret the Law. The number seventy would then mean that each mind interprets the Torah in its own way. In a more practical sense, rabbinic interpretation has been divided into four categories:

P'shat, the simple meaning, or Plain Sense
Drash, the homiletic meaning (from this, *MiDrash*)
Remez, the esoteric meaning
Sod, the hidden, kabbalistic, meaning

Of these, *P'shat,* Plain Sense, is the most readily understood and appreciated by the nonscholar. Nevertheless,
the work of correctly deciphering *P'shat* remains an ever-
challenging experience for the scholar as well.

P'shat is the basic meaning of the text. As the Sages
have taught, "No scriptural interpretation ever aban-
dons its *P'shat*—Plain Sense" (*Aiyn Mikra Yotzie M'dei
P'shuto*). This means that, no matter what other interpretive modes are brought to bear on the text, the sentence
always retains its Plain Sense and it must be reckoned
with. The Plain Sense of the Scripture is the straightforward meaning of the text. We comprehend this by
means of the accepted rules of grammar, language, compositional syntax, psychological insight, and a bit of common sense. These tools are within the reach of any
intelligent student.

The Levels of *P'shat*

By Plain Sense interpretation, we do not mean manifest
meaning as opposed to latent meaning; nor do we mean
surface as opposed to depth; nor unidimensional as opposed to multidimensional. We mean all these things.
A most important and exciting aspect of *P'shat,* little-
appreciated even by experienced students, is that *P'shat*
itself has various levels of interpretation. Even the Simple
(or Plain) Sense, when delved into, offers a profundity
well beyond the surface meaning. Because *P'shat* exists
on different levels of understanding and because these
levels are not mutually exclusive, any one sentence may
have several mutually compatible *P'shat* interpretations.
The *P'shat*-insights garnered by the classical interpreta-

tive methods are always evident in the text, though they are by no means self-evident.

Only by sensitizing ourselves to the nuances of the text do we gain entrance into this inner world of *P'shat*. By uncovering the various levels of biblical meaning, Torah study becomes an intellectually challenging and spiritually inspiring adventure. In this way, interpreting the Torah becomes both serious pursuit and pleasurable pastime, an ongoing engagement with a never-ending source of wisdom and sublime ideas.

Jacob and Esau—Personalities and Prototypes

As an illustration, let us look at the biblical description of Jacob and Esau. My point here is to compare an initial understanding of the story with the additional layers of understanding that are gained from a closer analysis of the text. Ultimately deeper understanding leads to appreciation of the significance of the story, of the message the Torah wants to convey.

The Torah's story of Esau selling his birthright to his twin brother, Jacob, is one of the most familiar episodes in the Bible. We can begin here to uncover the manifest and latent layers of the Torah's textual meaning and message. The following is from Genesis 25:24–34:

And when her days to bear were full, behold, there were twins in her womb. And the first went out red, all over like a hairy robe; they called his name Esau. And after that went his brother out, his hand seizing Esau's heel; and his name he called Jacob. And Isaac was sixty years old when she bare them. And the lads grew up, and Esau was a cunning hunter, a man of the field; but Jacob was a plain man abiding in tents. And Isaac loved Esau because he ate of his venison, but Rebecca loves Jacob. And Jacob sod pottage and Esau came from the field and he was tired, and Esau said to Jacob, Let me devour, I pray thee, from this red, red stuff for I am faint; therefore was his name called Edom. And Jacob said, Sell me this day your birth-right. And Esau said, Behold I am in peril to die, and what is this birthright to me? And Jacob said, Swear to me this day; and he swore to him; and he sold his birthright to Jacob. Then Jacob gave to Esau bread and pottage of lentils, and he did eat and drink, and he rose and went; and Esau despised his birthright.

This fateful deal between the brothers—birthright for a bowl of pottage—provokes uncomfortable moral questions which must be grappled with. But let us put them aside for the moment and look at another facet of this story.

The giving of names at birth in the Torah is usually associated with the events of birth or the character of the child. In this story, we see that Esau is given this name because he comes out of the womb fully developed with a complete coat of hair (*Esau* in Hebrew means "made," "finished"). Jacob's name comes from the fact that he grabbed onto the heel of his older brother (*Jacob* from the word "heel").

The meaning seems to be that Esau is already developed; the implication—that there will be no further development, he is static. For Jacob, the meaning seems to be that he is a reaching, actively striving individual; he is dynamic.

Yet when we meet the boys again after they have grown up, we find the very opposite. Esau is the hunter, man of the field—he is now the man of action—while Jacob is a man dwelling in tents, sedentary—he is now the passive one.

This characterization is once again reversed when we read of the sale of the birthright. Here we read that Esau is tired, faint, and, to his way of thinking, on the verge of death. Jacob, on the other hand, while engaged in the quiet domestic activity of cooking, is mentally active. He plans, he thinks of the future, he wants the birthright not for what it can give him today but for its significance for posterity. He has a vision of an unseen future. Esau, on the other hand, lacks vision; he can see but cannot perceive. He is located in the here and now.

> And Esau said to Jacob: Let me devour, I pray thee, from this red, red stuff for I am faint, *therefore was his name called Edom.*

The naming here is important. It comes in the same sentence as Esau's quote; this is a clue. It tells us the significance of Esau's apparently incidental remark. The question poses itself: Why, in fact, is this name chosen?

Why, of all words, should the word *Edom* ("red") stick to Esau and become his second name? Why not, for example, *Halietaine* ("let me devour")? Or *Nezid* ("pottage")? These would seem more reminiscent of the birthright-for-pottage sale. The Torah's point seems to be that this phrase and this word are particularly revealing of Esau's personality.

Esau is "turned on" by what he sees and the mere color of food ("this red, red stuff") elicits his uncontrolled appetite. Now, as we think of it, the color of food is its most superficial aspect; it is much less important than its taste, smell, or even its texture. Yet this sensual being is fixated on its color, the surface of things. This, more than anything else, symbolizes his character—easily ignited passion, the need for immediate gratification, superficial stimulation. All poetically summed up in the color itself—RED, with its universal connotation of passion. He is now Esau/Edom.

We have Jacob's forbearance and planning as a foil for Esau's impatience, superficiality, and inability to delay gratification. Knowing his brother's nature, Jacob stresses the here and now in his talk with him: "Sell me *today* . . . Swear to me *today*. . . ." The repeated emphasis on *today* is meant to connect with Esau's "now-impulse," as if to say: "Do it *now*. What will be tomorrow is unimportant."

We can now understand and reconcile the seeming contradictions in the Torah's characterizations of Esau, first as passive, then as active; and Jacob, first as active, then as passive. We realize that Esau's activity is for the fleeting moment and thus is ultimately static and moribund. Jacob's passivity (dwelling in tents) is a means for purposeful, mental activity; it is a reaching for the future, a striving for purpose over pleasure.

A Closer Look at the Text

The delineation of the boys' character comes to us from a reading of the text on one level. A closer reading will give us other dimensions of this characterization. Here we come to the difference between reading the Torah in the original Hebrew or in its English translations, because grammatical subtleties are sometimes difficult to translate.

The text says:

And Isaac loved Esau because he ate of his venison, but Rebecca loves Jacob.

The grammatical slip is glaring—Isaac *loved* Esau . . . Rebecca *loves* Jacob. All translations gloss over the difference in tense which appears in the Hebrew original. Apparently they do so in order to "clean up the text," make grammatical sense out of it, and eliminate the awkward "error." But can this be an error? It is hardly likely that such a gross faux pas would creep into the text.

We must take the text as it stands. Isaac's love of Esau is in the past tense; Rebecca's love of Jacob is in the present tense. The meaning confirms the Esau/Jacob dichotomy. Isaac's love, built as it is on temporary appetite, is transient. Rebecca's love is unconditional and thus eternally valid.

This idea finds its expression when the rabbis state in *Sayings of the Fathers* (chapter 5:19):

Any love that depends on a specific cause, when that cause is gone, the love is gone; but if it does not depend on a specific cause, it will never cease.

We see now that Esau's involvement in the present actually dooms him to the past. Jacob's vision of the future affords him an eternal present.

Again let us look at the text:

And he did eat and drink and he rose and went; and Esau despised the birthright.

Note the linguistic style the Torah employs to depict Esau's actions—machine-gun rapidity—ate, drank, rose, went. When we have such uninterrupted serial action, we realize that the acts were done without forethought. Esau's actions are automatic, unthinking, reflex-like. Such flagrant and callous disregard for the value of the birthright is certainly to "despise it." Again we see the nature of Esau's actions—they are reflexes, not reflective. For all their busy-ness, they are essentially static.

The closer reading of the Torah's words fleshes in the picture. Nothing in the text is to be taken for granted; each nuance adds to our understanding.

A Distal Look at the Text

When we step back from this particular episode between Jacob and Esau and encompass more of the Torah's text in our purview, we find additional support and additional understanding of the differences between these two personalities.

Isaac and Rebecca send Jacob to Padan-aram to Rebecca's family to find a wife, because the Canaanite women were immoral and unbefitting the family of Abraham and Isaac.

And Rebecca said to Isaac, My life is harassed because of the daughters of Heth (Canaan); if Jacob take a wife of the daughters of Heth, like the daughters of the land (Canaan), what is life to me? And Isaac called Jacob, and blessed him, and commanded him, and said unto him, Thou shalt not take a wife of the daughters of Canaan. . . . When Esau saw that Isaac blessed Jacob and sent him away to Padan-aram to take a wife from thence; and that as he blessed him, he prohibited him, saying, Thou shalt not take a wife of the daughters of Canaan . . . And Esau thus saw that the daughters of Canaan were evil in the eyes of Isaac his father. Then Esau went to Ishmael and took Mahalath the daughter of Ishmael, Abraham's son, the sister of Nebajoth, *in addition to his wives,* to be his wife. (Genesis 27:46 ff)

"In addition to his wives"!? The phrase is jarring. Didn't Esau realize that these women were evil in Isaac's eyes? Didn't he realize that marrying into Abraham's family was necessary mainly so as not to marry a Canaanite woman? It is clear from here that Esau didn't realize this. His superficiality and his sensuality—so clearly depicted in the pottage/birthright episode—took charge. His intoxication with surface meaning, with little comprehension of its inner significance, made his mistake inevitable. He saw Jacob go to the family to marry, so he too went to the family to marry. But his womanizing instincts wouldn't allow him to give up his previous wives, even though his father despised them, and so he took this new wife "in addition to his wives."

Our understanding of the man, Jacob, likewise finds confirmation when he too receives a second name, as did his brother, Esau/Edom.

Jacob wrestles with and overcomes an unknown "man" that attacks him while alone at night.

And he said to him: What is your name? And he said, Jacob. And he said, Thy name shall be called no more Jacob, but Israel; for you have striven (*sarisa*) with

God and with man and hast prevailed. (Genesis
32:27–28)

Jacob becomes Israel (*Sarisa,* "you strove")—the striv-
er, the survivor, the dynamic struggler. At birth he was
reaching, in his youth he was planning for the future, and
in his adulthood he was striving forward, overcoming
challenges.

Personalities Become Prototypes

The Torah-text finds many ways, both obvious and subtle,
to convey the multidimensionality of the different personalities of these two brothers. Jacob and Esau are the found-
ing fathers of separate peoples. These two peoples
represent two poles on the moral/spiritual continuum;
they represent two opposite approaches to living. One
proclaims the motto of the Now Generation, "I want
what I want when I want it"—in short, the sensate, sen-
suous being. The other is the future-oriented person for
whom the present is but a stepping stone to strive for some
distant value. For him, this world is but the antechamber
of the World-to-Come, as the Sages put it. One is tied to
this world and is thus mortal; the other, to the future
world, and thus immortal.

The Scriptures are not subtle as to which prototype is
preferred. The prophet Malachi spells it out for us:

I have loved you, saith the Lord.
Yet you say, Wherein hast Thou loved us?
Was not Esau Jacob's brother?
Yet I loved Jacob,

But Esau I hated.
(Malachi 1:2–3)

The Moral Question

But what of the disturbing, nagging question: How could Jacob be so immoral as to take cruel advantage of his famished brother and wring from him a concession of the birthright when the latter was on the verge of death? Is this the brotherly love the Torah wants to teach us? Is this behavior befitting the Father of the nation who were to be enjoined "Don't stand idly by when your neighbor is bleeding to death" (Leviticus 19:14). And, furthermore, what validity can such a coerced sale have?

Does our text in any way deal with these questions? We should not look for any obvious ethical discussion here. When the Torah teaches morality through narrative, it does so only in the most oblique manner.

Our analysis until now has by no means exhausted the text. There is an infinite quality to the Torah which promises unending discoveries if we but search for them. I will share with the reader several surprises which I came upon of late, the effect of which is to completely alter the thrust of this all-too-familiar story. Familiarity in this case is only a hindrance for it blinds us to the veiled layers of meaning contained within.

Once more, it is the close reading of the words of the Torah which is our guide, this being the necessary and sufficient tool for breaking open the secrets of the Torah.

Let's look at the very last sentence of the pottage/birthright episode once more.

Then Jacob gave to Esau bread and pottage of lentils,
and he did eat and drink, and he rose and went; and
Esau despised his birthright.

Our first surprise is that Jacob gave Esau bread in addition to the pottage; Esau had only asked for pottage ("this
red, red stuff"). Why the gratuitous gift?

The second surprise is that Jacob seems to have given
him something to drink as well, for does it not say "and
he did eat and drink . . ." Strange that no mention is made
in the text until now of Jacob giving Esau to drink. But he
did drink. This is one of many such instances in the Torah,
which indicates that much more goes on within the
Torah's episodes than is, in fact, recorded.

So, while Esau pleaded only for the bowl of pottage,
Jacob gave him pottage with a side portion of bread
and aperitif. It turns out that Jacob, our callous, calcu-
lating bargainer, is somewhat more magnanimous than
first suspected.

The next surprise is that Jacob *gave* Esau anything. Why
does the Torah say "gave"? Jacob didn't *give* anything, it
was a deal, pure and simple. A barter—birthright for
pottage. Jacob bought the birthright and sold the pottage;
Esau bought the pottage and sold the birthright. Jacob
sold to Esau is more accurate. Had not Jacob even said,
"Sell me today your birthright"? Why then the use of this
benign and misleading term?

Our last surprise as we study this final sentence closely
is the most startling of them all. It has the effect of provid-
ing a jolting denouement; the whole story is transposed,
standing it on its head and giving it an O. Henry twist.

Here our English translations utterly fail us. Knowledge
of biblical Hebrew is crucial. The English reads, "Then

Jacob gave to Esau. . . ." The Hebrew reads, "*V'Yaakov natan l''Esav,*" which, correctly translated, reads, "And Jacob had given to Esau. . . ." Hebrew has no special past participle tense ("he had done"). In the Bible, this is accomplished by reversing the verb/subject order. "And Jacob gave" in Hebrew would be *VaYiten Yaakov;* whereas, "Jacob had given" is *V'Yaakov natan,* which is precisely what we have here. See for example "Now Rachel had taken the teraphim" (Genesis 31:34), in Hebrew *V'Rachel lakcha et hatraphim.* Rashi makes this point on Genesis 4:1, "And Adam knew his wife Eve."

In adumbrated fashion our story now looks like this:

> And Jacob made pottage.
> And Esau came from the field.
> And Esau said, Let me devour.
> And Jacob said, Sell me today.
> And Esau said, Behold I am going to die.
> And Jacob said, Swear to me today.
> And he swore and he sold his birthright.
> *Now Jacob had given Esau bread and pottage.*
> And Esau ate and drank and rose and went away.
> And Esau despised the birthright.

The sense here is that Jacob had already given the food to Esau before their discussion of the birthright and its sale. Needless to say, this is radically different from our first impression of the events of this story. The picture we now get is that when Esau came in from the field and asked to devour the red, red stuff, Jacob *gave* it to him immediately, with bread and drink to boot. And while Esau was engrossed in wolfing down his food, Jacob brought up the topic of the birthright and offered to buy it from his brother (for cash, we can assume). Esau couldn't be bothered with such inanities for he was going to die, in any event. So he cavalierly sold it to Jacob. And thus Esau despised his birthright!

With this interpretation, offered by the *Hak'tav V'Hakabbalah,* the question of the morality of the pottage/birthright sale evaporates. Not only had Jacob not taken advantage of the desperate Esau, he had, instead, graciously served him. Only later did they work out a deal about the birthright. The fact that Esau would sell his birthright while under no duress only highlights the last words of our text, "And Esau did despise the birthright."

The reader might protest that we have prettified the story. But this interpretation, in fact, has told it as it is. The text bears it out. That this jars our accustomed way of understanding the story only highlights the importance of approaching the Torah-text with openness and without preconceived notions. Well, you say, if Jacob was really in the right in this case, what can we say about him deceiving his blind father, Isaac, and stealing the blessing intended for Esau? Ah . . . but that's another story!

The above analysis of a well-known chapter in the Torah exemplifies the in-depth approach to understanding the Torah which this book advocates. Three characteristics central to this approach can be discerned in the analysis.

1. The *P'shat,* Plain Sense, interpretation is based exclusively on the text. Every Plain Sense interpretation must find its validation within the text itself.

A twelfth-century Torah commentator, Rabbi Yosef Krah, put it succinctly: "When the Scriptures were written, they were written complete with all their solutions and all that was necessary so that future generations should not stumble in them. Nothing is lacking in their place, there being no need to bring proof from another place nor from the Midrash. . . ."

The text itself contains all we need to know for a thorough, rational understanding of its message.

2. A close study of the text, by means of the rules of Plain Sense textual interpretation, will reveal meanings not initially apparent. This means that *P'shat* itself is amenable to deeper and deeper levels of understanding. These understandings at times enrich and deepen our first impressions and, at other times (like the case above), completely alter our understanding. The astounding reality is that the Bible remains, even after thousands of years of intensive interpretation, an infinite repository of new insights.

3. These Plain Sense interpretations offer new, meaningful insights, insights of significance. *P'shat* deals with understanding the text correctly, whether the issue is a linguistic, historic, theological, or halachic one. There are certainly isolated interpretations of limited import. But the main benefit of in-depth *P'shat* interpretation is to discover matters of substance, discoveries that reflect and reveal philosophic, religious, ethical, and psychological insights of consequence. By means of these interpretations, we sense the sublimity of the Torah's wisdom, wisdom that has not dimmed over the three thousand years of its existence. It is the attainment of this wisdom which makes study of the Scriptures so challenging. It is the discovery of such insights which makes the endeavor such a spiritually and intellectually rewarding experience.

3
Key 1—Opening Sentences

Sentences that introduce sections in the Torah often convey more information than is apparent at first glance. These sentences can set the tone for the ensuing section, whether it be of a narrative or halachic character. The sensitive reader will pay close attention to the nuances in these sentences for clues which reveal either a motif, an important emphasis, or the main message of the passage. Interpreting the layers of meaning in these sentences is our first Key to understanding the Torah's messages.

First, a word about the divisions and subdivisions in the Torah. The Torah scroll has no chapter divisions. The chapter divisions of the Torah and Prophets, as we know them, are a medieval Christian idea. If we were to open a Torah scroll, we would find three types of divisions. The shortest is the closed *Parsha* ("section"), meaning that there is a blank space of nine letter lengths which separates sections. The next larger division is that of the open *Parsha*. This is similar to our paragraph in that it always begins on a new line. Then there is the largest division, which divides each of the five Books of Moses. These are separated by several blank lines.

With no vowelizing or punctuation in the Torah scroll, even sentences are not marked off as independent units. These divisions are known to us by way of the Oral Massoretic tradition.

The Opening Sentences that I am referring to are sentences that are found at the beginning of closed or open *Parshiot,* or at the beginning of one of the Books.

Let us see what this Key to Interpretation can do for us in our analysis of the Torah text.

The following example, which introduces a narrative section, illustrates how a clue embedded in the opening sentence reveals the moral message of the entire passage.

Example 1—A Matter of Priorities

In the Book of Numbers, we read how the tribes of Reuben and Gad request permission from Moses to remain in Transjordan and not cross over into the Land of Canaan with the rest of the nation.

Chapter 32 begins: "And much cattle was had to the children of Reuben and to the children of Gad, a very great multitude; and when they saw the land Jazer and the land of Gilead, that, behold the place was a place for cattle."

A first reading informs us that these tribes had much cattle and, because of this, they made a claim to remain in Transjordan, a "place for cattle."

A closer reading discloses several unusual stylistic nuances. N. Leibowitz has noted the striking construction of this sentence. In the Hebrew, the very same word "cattle" both opens and closes the sentence. This is truly remarkable and may be the only such instance in the whole Scriptures. In this case, the tribes' obsession with their cattle is graphically expressed.

Close inspection of this ordinary-looking sentence uncovers another nuance. The sentence begins with the words "And much cattle" and only later tells us who the owners are—"the children of Reuben and Gad." It would read more smoothly to say simply, "And the children of Reuben . . . had much cattle." In fact, this is the translation we find in all English Bibles. Yet it is not precise and it blurs the subtle message of the Hebrew text.

Compare this with the story of Abraham and his nephew Lot. There we read: "And Abram was very rich in cattle, in silver, and in gold" (Genesis 13:2). Here Abraham, the possessor, comes first and then the listing of his possessions. In our case of Reuben and Gad, their possessions come first before they themselves are mentioned.

This stylistic reversal alerts us to a reversal of priorities. And *that* is the underlying message of this story: the children of Reuben and the children of Gad have elevated the importance of material possessions above that of personal worth. This becomes evident as we review the whole chapter. Note the following:

And they stepped near to him and said, We will build sheepfolds for our cattle and cities for our little ones (Numbers 32:16).

Moses recognized this perverse reversal of priorities (cattle before children) and corrected them:

Build cities for your little ones and folds for your
sheep (Numbers 32:24).

That this moral message is picked up by the tribes we
can see from their answer to Moses: "And the children of
Gad and the children of Reuben said to Moses, Your
servants will do as my lord has said. *Our children, our
wives, and our cattle* and all our animals will remain
there in the cities of Gilead." Note the immediate correc-
tion of priorities.

Note also that the children of Reuben and Gad barely
mention God's name when they speak to Moses. "We will
equip and speed *before the children of Israel* . . ."
(Numbers 32:17). Again Moses corrects them: "If you will
do this thing, if you will equip *before God* to war" (Numbers 32:20). Moses is telling them that their obligation is
foremost to God and then to their brothers, the children
of Israel. They have again reversed priorities.

Now take a look at the next section and notice a remarkable thing:

And Moses said to them: If you do this thing, if
you will arm yourselves to go *before the Lord* to
the war, And every armed man of you will pass over
the Jordan *before the Lord,* until He has driven
out His enemies from before Him, And the land be
subdued *before the Lord* and you return afterward;
then you shall be clear from the Lord and before
Israel and this land shall be unto you for a possession *before the Lord.* But if you will not do so,
behold, you have sinned against the Lord; and know
you your sin which will find you. Build you cities
for your little ones and folds for your sheep and

do that which has proceeded out of your mouth. And the children of Gad and the children of Reuben spoke unto Moses saying: Your servants will do as my lord commands. Our little ones, our wives, our flocks, and all our cattle shall be there in the cities of Gilead; But thy servants will pass over, every man that is armed for war, *before the Lord,* to battle as my lord said. So Moses gave charge concerning them to Eleazar the priest and to Joshua, the son of Nun, and to the heads of the fathers' houses of the tribes of the children of Israel. And Moses said to them: If the children of Gad and the children of Reuben will pass with you over the Jordan every man that is armed to battle, *before the Lord,* and the land shall be subdued before you, then you shall give them the land of Gilead for a possession. But if they will not pass over with you armed, they shall have possessions among you in the land of Canaan. And the children of Gad and the children of Reuben answered, saying: As the Lord has said unto your servants, so will we do. We will pass over armed *before the Lord* unto the land of Canaan and the possession of our inheritance shall remain with us beyond the Jordan. (Numbers 32:20–32)

The words "before God" appear seven times in this section (see the chapter on the Seven Code). This is the Torah's way of emphasizing a point. The theme is clear: Moses is teaching the children of Gad and Reuben a lesson in value priorities. People come before cattle and God comes before people! This is the message of the chapter and its motif can already be found in the opening sentence.

Halachic (legal) sections also have introductory sentences which have to be read carefully to mine their full meaning.

Example 2—"If You Buy a Hebrew Servant . . ."

The laws of the Hebrew servant were given immediately after the Revelation at Sinai, not long after the Exodus from Egypt. They are found in Exodus, chapter 21: "If you buy a Hebrew servant, six years shall he serve; and in the seventh he shall go out free for nothing."

This section obviously teaches us the laws of the Hebrew servant. But a closer look shows us the particular emphasis the Torah places on the servant's "going out free."

The section continues:

If he came in by himself, he shall *go out* by himself; if he be married, then his wife shall *go out* with him. If his lord has given him a wife and she bore him sons or daughters, the wife and her children shall be her lord's and he shall *go out* by himself. And if the servant shall plainly say, I love my lord, my wife, and my children, I shall not *go out* free. Then his lord shall cause him to step unto the judges, he shall also cause him to step to the door or to the doorpost, and his lord shall bore his ear through with an awl, and he shall serve him for ever. And, if a man sell his daughter to be a maidservant, she shall not *go out* as the menservants do. If she be evil in the eyes of her lord who has betrothed her to himself, then shall he let her be released, to sell her to an alien people he shall have no power, seeing he has dealt deceitfully with her. And if he has betrothed her to his son, he shall do unto her after the manner of daughters. If he take him another, her sustenance, her raiment, and her duty of marriage shall he not diminish. And if he do not these three unto her, then shall she *go out free* without money. (Exodus 21:2–11)

While this section tells us about the laws of the Hebrew servant, only a particular aspect of those laws is discussed here. We are not told the laws regarding purchasing a Hebrew servant, nor how a master should treat his servant, nor what a servant's obligations to his master are. The message behind these laws is of another nature. It clearly is: If you purchase a servant, uppermost in your mind should be the matter of setting him free. Freeing one's servant is the theme drummed home here. And this can be seen already from the opening sentence: it is conditional—*If* you buy a Hebrew servant . . . *then* he shall go out free. Thus the first sentence contains the main theme of this law section.

Note also that the words "go out" appear exactly seven times in this section—again, an indication that this is the lesson the Torah wants to emphasize. This is a fitting introduction to the Israelites' rule of law after their redemption from the backbreaking experience of Egyptian slavery.

The laws of the Hebrew servant are also dealt with in another section of the Torah. Comparing these two sections will give us an insight into the Torah's style and how it conveys different latent messages within similar manifest content.

Example 3—"If Your Brother . . . Is Sold to You . . ."

In Leviticus 25:39, we find: "And if your brother who is *with you* be waxen poor and be sold to you, you shall not compel him to serve as a bond servant."

This opening sentence has a different emphasis from the one in Exodus. Here, its message is: Don't maltreat your servant, don't put him in bondage. The rest of the section continues:

As a hired worker and as a sojourner he shall be *with you* and shall serve *with you* unto the year of the Jubilee. And then he shall go away from being *with you,* both he and his children *with him,* and shall return unto his own family and unto the possession of his fathers shall he return. For they are my servants, whom I brought forth from the land of Egypt; they shall not be sold as bondsmen. You shall not rule over him with rigor, but shall fear your God. Both your manservant and your maidservant who shall be yours shall be of the nations that are round about you; of them you may buy menservants and maidservants. Moreover of the children of the tolerated strangers that do sojourn *with you,* of them you may buy and of their families that are *with you* which they begat in your land, and they shall be your possession. And you may leave them as an inheritance for your children after you, to inherit them for a possession; they shall serve you forever, but over your brothers, the children of Israel, you shall not rule over one another with rigor.

The ear attuned to the music of the Torah's words notices the sevenfold use of the term "with you (him)." How apt a phrase to convey the message that this servant is no less a human being than is his master; treat him as an equal because he is "with you," equal to you.

We see how two similar legal sections emphasize different aspects of the law. Equally significant, we see how the opening sentence in each case highlights the basic message of each section.

I have shown how this particular Key to Interpretation (Opening Sentences) was reinforced by the use of another, more subtle, Key, that of the Seven Code (see chapter 10). The comparison of the two sections should make it clear that our interpretation is not an arbitrary one. The Keys have helped us uncover the message beneath the surface text.

Let us look at a more obvious example:

Example 4—"Isaac Was Old and His Eyes Were Too Dim . . ."

Introducing the story of Isaac blessing his sons, we read: "And it came to pass that when Isaac was old and his eyes were too dim to see, he called Esau his oldest son and said to him, My son: and he said to him, Behold here am I" (Genesis 27:1).

The story that follows tells us how Rebecca took advantage of Isaac's poor eyesight and sent Jacob, the younger son, into his father's chamber to receive the blessing intended for Esau.

It is clear then that Isaac's dim eyes are to play the key role in the story of the stolen blessings. Note also that by placing the statement about Isaac's dim eyes in the same sentence with his calling his son, the Torah is giving us a clue that there is a causal relationship between these two facts. Let us look at another example with a less obvious message.

Example 5—The Man Moses

The Torah introduces the adult Moses with the following sentence:

"And it came to pass in those days, when Moses was grown, that he went out unto his brothers and saw their burdens, and he saw an Egyptian man smiting a Hebrew man, one of his brothers" (Exodus 2:11).

The sentence is noteworthy because it is the first mention of Moses as an adult. The Torah chooses to point out one act of Moses, that he went out to see the burdens of his brothers. This choice is certainly not an arbitrary one. It tells us something very important about the most towering figure of the Torah. Moses identified with the sufferings of his brothers, even though he himself, coming from Pharaoh's house, was not subject to these sufferings. This empathy for suffering turns out to be a very basic character trait of Moses. It manifests itself over and over again throughout the Torah.

We are immediately told of three cases where Moses intervened to save the underdog. First, he saves a Jew from the hands of his Egyptian taskmaster, then he prevents a Jew from being victimized by a fellow Jew, and, last, he rescues the daughters of Jethro from the bullying Midian shepherds.

When Pharaoh increases the workload of the Jews, after Moses had gone to him and asked him to free his people, Moses cries out to God in desperation: "Why have you done such evil to this people?" (Exodus 5:22). Later, during their wanderings in the wilderness, the Jews cry out for meat and, in his frustration, Moses pleads with God, "And if You will do this for me, please kill me, if I have found favor in Your eyes, and let me not see my evil (Rashi's reading, 'their' evil)." He prefers death to witnessing their suffering. It is clear that this causes him palpable pain.

The thrust of this opening sentence, by pointing out Moses' deeply felt empathy for the victims of injustice, conveys the message that this character trait was the reason he was chosen to lead his people. His deeply felt concern for their burdens qualified him above all others for the monumental task of leading the Jewish people out of slavery and to the Revelation at Mt. Sinai.

The word Torah derives from the Hebrew word *Hora'ah,* which means "teaching." The Torah teaches in all its forms, whether they be narrative, poetic, legal, or historical. Its *raison d'etre* is to teach. And its most powerful lessons are its most subtle ones. These subtle messages can more easily be detected when we closely analyze "Opening Sentences"; each carries its own motif. This can be our key to understanding the passage as a whole.

4

Key 2—The Contiguity Principle

Meaning is always derived from its context. We can no more understand the meaning of a word isolated from its sentence than we can appreciate a musical note torn from its melody. Earlier, I suggested the meta-principle in Torah interpretation of Text-in-Context, meaning that interpretation begins with viewing the text within its larger context. This is our first clue to discovering the meaning of individual words, phrases, whole sentences, and larger sections in the Torah.

What I call the Contiguity Principle—deriving interpretive clues from the neighboring text—is the more focused application of this larger meta-principle. As I have shown with the illustration of the case of Joseph choosing Simeon to incarcerate (chapter 1), the application of this commonsense principle is not always that obvious. Our first benefit from this principle arises when we become consciously aware of its importance and its relevance. Awareness enables us to scrutinize the text in ways that lead to new understandings, as when continued scrutiny of the figure–ground illusion enables us to see new configurations within a familiar pattern. And, just as with the figure–ground example, once we gain a new perspective, it is difficult ever again to see things as we did before.

I personally have been amazed by the insights this simple rule can uncover.

Example 1—"The Serpent Was More Subtle . . ."

In Genesis 3:1–6, we read:

Now the serpent was more subtle than any other animal of the field which the Lord God had made. And it said to the woman, Although God hath said, Ye shall not eat of every tree of the garden. . . . And the woman said unto the serpent, We may eat of the fruit of the trees of the garden; But of the fruit of the tree which is in the midst of the garden, God hath said, Ye shall not eat of it, neither shall ye touch it, lest ye die. And the serpent said unto the woman, Ye shall not surely die; For God doth know that in the day ye eat thereof, then your eyes shall be opened, and ye shall be as gods, knowing good and evil. And when the woman saw that the tree was good for food, and that it was a delight to the eyes, and a tree to be desired in order to make one wise, she took of the fruit thereof, and did eat, and gave also to her husband with her; and he did eat.

The tale is straightforward enough. The serpent talks Eve ("the woman") into eating from the forbidden fruit. But some things are not clear. The serpent is introduced as the "most subtle" of all animals. But where is his subtlety evidenced in this story? Another problem is in the woman's response to the serpent. She says: "God hath said, Ye shall not eat of it, neither shall ye touch it, lest ye die." But this is not what God said. He only forbade eating of the fruit; touching wasn't mentioned at all. Why, we ask, would Eve add this prohibition?

We can take it as a given that the serpent's subtlety wouldn't have been mentioned were it not integral to the story. Yet what the serpent said was not particularly subtle or sly. What he said was quite to the point, that this was a Tree of Knowledge of Good and Evil and that knowledge would make man similar to God. He was just "telling it as it is."

With the Contiguity Principle in mind, we would look at the neighboring information given in the sentence where the serpent's subtlety is mentioned. What does it say? "Now the serpent was more subtle than any animal of the field which the Lord God had made. *And he said unto the woman, Although God hath said, Ye shall not eat of every tree of the garden.* . . ." In the original Hebrew this is all one sentence. His opening words to Eve are placed within the same sentence as the fact of his subtleness. This is a clue. It points to relatedness, either causal or correlational, between the two parts of the sentence. He was subtle and he said . . .

The serpent was, in fact, quite clever. He used what modern psychologists call "reframing." By exaggerating the actual prohibition (from one tree to "every tree of the garden"), he created a new, but lopsided, frame of reference. He anticipated Eve's rebuttal, "we may eat of the trees of the garden," but in so doing he pulled her off balance. Her opposition to him on this point made her more vulnerable to exaggerate herself ("we may not eat neither may we touch it"). People have a natural tendency to do this in order to relieve the tension of overt conflict. By lessening the gap between opposing positions, we soften the uneasiness of disagreement. (Merchants use this all the time in the *Shuk,* exaggerating prices to start with, so that the bargaining has enough room for "compromise." The potential buyer moves closer to his position to lessen disagreement. In the end, the crafty merchant gets the price he really wanted all along.)

Notice that the serpent doesn't even finish his sentence. He waits to draw the woman into his trap. And she fell for it!

The Torah is subtle about the serpent's subtleness. But it's all there before our eyes. The neighboring (contiguous) phrase casts light on its meaning.

Example 2—"And the Spirit of Jacob Their Father Was Revived"

This passage is the culmination of Jacob's twenty-two year mourning for his long-lost son, Joseph. Yet there is something strange about the passage. After the brothers went down to Egypt and after the unrecognized Joseph put his brothers through a series of challenges, he revealed himself to them, to their utter disbelief. Having convinced them that he was indeed the brother they sold into slavery, he sent them back to their father, Jacob, to tell him that he is alive, to relate "all his glory in Egypt," and to bring Jacob down to Egypt.

> And they [brothers] told him, saying, Joseph is yet alive, and he is ruler over all the land of Egypt. And Jacob's heart went cold, for he did not believe them. And they spoke to him all the words of Joseph, which he had said to them; and when he saw the wagons that Joseph had sent to bear him, the spirit of Jacob their father was revived. (Genesis 45:26–27)

The question that begs to be asked is: what brought about Jacob's sudden change of heart? From not believing his sons' wild story, he suddenly accepted it as true and "his spirit is revived."

The words immediately preceding this statement read "and Jacob saw the wagons that Joseph sent to bear him. . . ." This is our clue. Why would seeing the wagons which Joseph sent "revive Jacob's spirit" and convince him that, in fact, Joseph is alive?

Rashi approaches this question and answers it with an aggadic interpretation. But the Plain Sense interpretation can be deduced from a close examination of the context. When his sons told him that Joseph was alive and living in Egypt, he didn't believe them because he had no way of verifying their unbelievable story. But once Jacob saw the wagons that would take him down to Egypt, he was certain that this was no fabrication, for could he not now see for himself? The next sentence validates this interpretation: "And Israel said: It is enough; Joseph my son is yet alive. *I will go and see him before I die.*"

Our Key to Understanding here is the contiguous text, that is, the words preceding and following the puzzling statement of Jacob's revived spirits.

Example 3—The Birth of Moses

"And the woman was pregnant and bare a son: and when she saw that he was good, she concealed him for three months" (Exodus 2:2).

The first question that comes to mind is: What did Moses' mother see that made her conclude that he was good? Aren't all babies "good" in the eyes of their mothers? Certainly they are "good" if the alternative is drowning them. The statement is gratuitous. What then is its purpose? The Contiguity Principle can disclose a simple, sensible explanation.

In analyzing the text, we see that this complex sentence has several parts to it: (1) Pregnancy and birth of Moses, (2) his mother sees that he is good, and (3) she decides to hide him from the Egyptians.

The eleventh-century commentator, Rabbi Elazar of Worms, reminds us that human nature doesn't change. He says what parents throughout the ages know, that a quiet baby is a "good baby." The newborn infant is good if he doesn't cry. The sentence now fits together as a whole: "And she saw that he was good (i.e., quiet) and she was thus able to conceal him." The beauty of the interpretation is in its simplicity.

The classical commentators, "pursuers of *P'shat*," were exquisitely sensitive to the juxtaposition of two apparently unrelated phrases in the same sentence. At times, this would give rise to some unexpected interpretations. See what this does to the biblical basis for the familiar milk and meat injunction.

Example 4—"Thou Shalt Not Seethe a Kid . . ."

"The first of the first fruits of thy ground thou shalt bring to the house of the Lord thy God; Thou shalt not seethe a kid in its mother's milk" (Exodus 23:19).

This injuction forbidding seething a kid in its mother's milk is the biblical basis for the laws of *Kashruth* requiring the separation of meat and milk. See how the following Plain Sense interpretation, based on the Contiguity Principle, completely divests this clause of that familiar meaning.

At first glance, we have here two unrelated clauses within the same sentence. Not so, according to the early commentator Joseph Bekhor Shor. He points out that the word *Bashail,* regularly translated here as "seethe," really means "to become ripe or mature." The phrase then means "Thou shalt not allow a kid to become mature with its mother's milk," that is, you should not allow the kid to mature, rather bring it as a sacrifice in the Temple. In this way, both clauses of the sentence are related: Bring your first fruits as an offering and likewise bring your first—young—animals as offerings to God.

The previous example illustrates how a Plain Sense interpretation may run counter to an accepted halachic

interpretation. Yet the Contiguity Principle may be used
to explicate legal injunctions as well.

In the Ten Commandments, we have a clear division
between those *mitzvot* which are between man and God
and those in the second tablet containing *mitzvot* between man and man. The second tablet reads:

Example 5—"Thou Shalt Not Steal"

"Thou shalt not murder; Thou shalt not commit adultery;
Thou shalt not steal; Thou shalt not bear false witness
against thy fellowman" (Exodus 20:13).

The talmudic Sages determined that the prohibition
against stealing here refers to kidnapping, "stealing people," and not stealing property or money. Their guide was
the Contiguity Principle. They reasoned that, since the
prohibitions against murder and adultery, the two preceding commandments, are punishable by death, then so, too,
must be the prohibition to steal, which follows them. This
could only mean kidnapping, since stealing money is never
punishable by death. Thus, the immediate textual context
of the command sheds light on its meaning.

The Contiguity Principle is known in rabbinic literature
as *Smichut Parshiot* ("adjacent sections"). This means
that two apparently unrelated sections in the Torah are
placed in juxtaposition to teach some moral lesson. The
interpretation thus derived is usually of an aggadic, not
Plain Sense, nature.

As an example, in Numbers 5:11–31, we find that the
laws of the *Sota* (wife suspected of having relations with
another man) are immediately followed by the laws of the

Nazarite (Numbers 6:1–21). The midrashic comment on this is "Why is the section dealing with the Nazarite placed in juxtaposition to the section dealing with the *Sota?* To teach you that he who sees the *Sota* in her disgrace should abstain from wine, because it may lead to adultery."

What I have called the Contiguity Principle is an extention of this idea used to derive the Plain Sense of the text by analysis of its immediate context, both between sentences and within sentences. It is, as I have shown, a powerful tool for this purpose.

5

Key 3—Similarities between Different Texts

It has been said that a sign of the creative individual is his ability to perceive the differences in similar things and the similarities in different things. This is true for interpretation in the Torah as well. Finding these similarities and differences is a real challenge to our ability to understand the meaning of the Torah-text, to plumb its depths, and to interpret its messages.

The Torah is a unified document. At the same time, it is a large variegated tapestry, an intricate masterpiece with different patterns woven into it. Yet, for all that, it remains a cohesive whole. This means, in effect, that to be able to fully understand any one section of the Torah, one must be familiar with all its sections. This is a daunting task. The talmudic Sages and the classical Torah commentators were intimately familiar with all parts of the Scriptures, which made them eminently qualified to interpret them. We can learn from their insights; their interpretations are our guide in our attempts to understand the Torah's many levels of meaning.

Similarities

Rare words or phrases which appear in different sections of the Torah, no matter how far separated, may be used as connecting links between the two sections. By tying together two apparently unrelated and separated sections by means of a verbal association, the Torah creates an opportunity for us to become aware of a deeper message. Without noticing the verbal bridge, we would entirely miss the message. Examples of the meanings transported by these verbal bridges are part of our In-Depth Interpretation of the story of Joseph (chapter 12). Following are other instances of this interpretative Key—how similar words or phrases in different parts of the Bible enlighten us as to their deeper meaning.

Example 1—The Inheritance of the Priests

In Genesis, chapter 47, we are told that the Egyptians are forced to sell their land to Joseph for food during the years of famine. But Joseph did not buy the land of the priests "For the priests had a portion from Pharaoh and did eat their portion which Pharaoh gave them; *therefore (Al Kain)* they sold not their land" (Genesis 47:22). So the Egyptian priests were privileged characters; they alone were entitled to hold on to land.

Compare this with what the Torah tells us about the Jewish priests: "Because [of] the tithing of the children of Israel, which they offer up to the Lord, I have given to the Levites for an inheritance; *therefore (Al Kain),* I have said to them, in the midst of the children of Israel *they shall not inherit an inheritance*'' (Numbers 18:24).

The contrast is striking. The precise reason justifying the holding of land by the Egyptian priests is the reason for the Jewish priests *not* to be landholders!

That this is not just a casual or fortuitous parallelism can be seen by comparing it with: ''*Therefore (Al Kain) the Levi had not a portion and an inheritance with his brothers*'' (Deuteronomy 10:9).

The Jewish priest must not have a material inheritance, for his life is devoted to spiritual pursuits. The Egyptian priest, on the other hand, is entitled to material benefits precisely because of his religious status. This contrast is brought to our notice by the use of the similar term *Al Kain;* it is a connecting phrase that makes us aware of the true difference between the two priestly castes. Notice how the term *Al Kain* bridges several different books of the Torah, tying together one thought.

Certain aspects of the Torah's unique style may not always be familiar to us even though we fully understand the Hebrew text. By becoming familiar with its communicative style, attuning ourselves to similar verbal phrases, across the five Books of the Torah (and across the Scriptures as a whole), we can see meanings that would otherwise have escaped us.

Example 2—Stylistic Idiosyncrasies and Interpretation

In Deuteronomy 5:3, we find a most startling statement. Moses is speaking to the Jewish people about the covenant at Sinai. He says:

Not with our fathers did the Lord make this covenant,
but with us, even us, who are all of us here alive today.

At this point, Moses was speaking to the Israelites at
the end of their forty years of wandering in the wilderness. These were the second generation, those born in
the wilderness. In light of this, we can see how strange
this phrase is. In fact, God *did* speak to their fathers at
Sinai *and not to them!* Our text says exactly the opposite.
How are we to understand this? The text has stumped
many commentators.

However, this style of "not . . . X (Not with our fathers . . .) but Y . . . (with us)" is not a one-time occur-
rence. Phrases similar to it in style occur throughout the
Torah and Prophets. They, too, can be quite puzzling.
Following are several of them:

1. After Joseph reveals to his brothers that he is their
long-lost brother, he says: "So now it was *not you* that
sent me here, *but God* . . ." (Genesis 45:8). Indeed! Was
it not them? Did they not throw him into the pit? Did they
not sell him to the passing Ishmaelites? Joseph himself
says, several sentences previously, "I am Joseph your
brother, whom *you sold* into Egypt . . ."(Genesis 45:4)!

2. Jacob struggles with the angel (Genesis 32:24–29)
and is told, "And he said: *Not Jacob* shall your name be
called any more, *but Israel,* for you have contended with
God and with men and have prevailed" (Genesis 32:28).
But, in spite of this explicit change of name, the Torah
continues to call Jacob, "Jacob"! The very next sentence
says, "And Jacob called the name of the place Peniel."
And, further on, we have "And God said to Israel in the
visions of the night and said 'Jacob, Jacob,' and he said:

'Here am I' " (Genesis 46:2). God Himself refers to Israel as Jacob!

3. A statement by the prophet Jeremiah has given classical commentators a difficult time. Jeremiah says, "For *I spoke not* unto your fathers, *nor commanded* them in the day that I brought them out of Egypt concerning burnt offerings and sacrifices. *But this thing did I command* them, saying, Listen to my voice, and I shall be for you for a God and you shall be for me for a nation . . . " (Jeremiah 7:22–23).

But had not God spoken to them about sacrifices? The covenant at Sinai was accompanied by sacrifices; the tabernacle was constructed for the sole purpose of bringing sacrifices; the Book of Leviticus is devoted to the laws of sacrifices. What could Jeremiah have meant by his statement?

The talmudic sages (*Brachot* 12) have cleared up these difficulties by pointing out a unique characteristic of biblical linguistic style. If we take this phrase literally, we have misunderstood it. Phrases constructed in the style of "Not . . . x, But . . . y . . ." do not mean "NOT X, But Y." Instead they mean: "Not X *is the main thing,* but rather Y is the main thing." Let us see how this simple change, which is consistent throughout the Scripture, helps us better understand these puzzling texts.

When Moses speaks to the second generation of the wilderness and says, "Not with our fathers did He make the covenant, but with us, here living today." This means "Not with our fathers *mainly* did he make a covenant, but with us—the living." Of course, we can see that the covenant has no meaning for history if it was given only, or even mainly, to the Jews at the time of Sinai;

rather, its purpose is to be a covenant to all Jews living in each generation.

Likewise, "Your name shall no longer be called Jacob (*mainly*), but Israel is your (*main*) name." Compare this with the similar, but different, name change in the case of Abraham. There his name is changed from Abram to Abraham and *never* again is he called Abram. "And thy name shall *not* be called any more Abram, *and* thy name shall be Abraham" (Genesis 17:5). Notice the precision of the Torah's choice of words: here it does not say, "Not Abram, But Abraham." It says instead, "*Not* Abram, *and* thy name shall be Abraham." The "Not . . . x, But . . . y" formula is absent and thus the meaning is different. The word "but" is replaced by the word "and," which implies "and in the future it will be Abraham."

Jeremiah was also pointing out that God did not command the sacrifices to be the *main* aspect of the Jew's life, but, rather, "listening to His voice" is the essence of the Torah.

Hearing the similar ring in these recurring phrases scattered throughout the Scriptures enables us to sense its true meaning. This meaning makes the Torah's message comprehensible. In this case, the medium is the message. The ear attuned to the verbal similarities across different texts picks it up.

Misinterpreting breeds misunderstanding. Sometimes small misunderstandings cast giant shadows.

Example 3—An Eye for an Eye

One of the most notorious injunctions is the biblical law of "an eye for an eye," known in academic circles as *lex talionis.* Several times in the Torah this law is stated; the first instance is from Exodus 21:22–25:

> And if men strive and hurt a woman with child so that she have a miscarriage, yet no harm follows, he shall surely be fined, according as the husband of the wife will lay upon him; and he shall give as the judges determine. But if there be harm then you shall give soul for soul. Eye for eye, tooth for tooth, hand for hand, foot for foot. Burn for burn, wound for wound, bruise for bruise.

Rabbinic Judaism has always interpreted the "eye for eye" law not in its literal sense but rather as monetary compensation for the victim's loss. However, many see this as apologetic revisionism. The contention is that, in fact, the Torah intended the courts to literally extract an eye for an eye from the wrongdoer. This cruel, sadistic, wasteful punishment has probably been the most outstanding blemish on the biblical system of justice.

A careful look at the text will, I think, show most unequivocally that the clear intention of the Torah was never the sadistic interpretation commonly conceived. I will analyze this from several angles. First, a broader view of the text:

> And if men quarrel and a man smite his fellow with a stone or with his fist and he die not, but keepth his bed; If he rise and walk outside upon his staff, then shall he that smote him be freed; he shall only pay for the loss of his time, and he shall cause him to be thoroughly healed. (Exodus 21:18–19)

A few sentences later, we find our text:

And if men strive and hurt a woman with child so that she have a miscarriage, yet no harm follows, he shall surely be fined, according as the husband of the wife will lay upon him; and he shall give as the judges determine. But if there be harm, then you shall give soul for soul. Eye for eye, tooth for tooth, hand for hand, foot for foot. Burn for burn, wound for wound, bruise for bruise. (Exodus 21:22–25)

Note that the first case is one of willfully inflicted harm, the second is of accidentally inflicted harm to the woman. By what logic could one explain that *accidental* harm is "recompensed" with an eye for an eye, while *willful* damage is punished by "*only* paying for the loss of time and he shall thoroughly be healed"! Certainly, if the intentional wrongdoer only has to pay for his victim's sick leave and medical expenses, then the hapless fellow who accidentally harmed this woman wouldn't be dealt with so vengefully.

There is a certain logic here which speaks for itself. A close look at the text itself also supports this idea. "But if there be harm *you shall give* (Hebrew: *v'natatah*) soul for soul, eye for eye. . . ."

Were the text's intention to extract an eye from the villain, the use of the word "give" is inappropriate. The *lex talionis* punishment is meant to take from the guilty, not to give to the victim. Certainly the victim has no desire to *receive* a gouged-out eye. It should have said, "and you shall *take* an eye for eye. . . ." But it doesn't; it says "give." Giving implies something that is meant to reach the recipient. Monetary compensation fits that definition; handing over a dismembered limb doesn't.

Again we refer to the text, this time in the original Hebrew. "Eye for (*tachat*) eye." The crucial word is *tachat*. Here is an instance where noting similarities between different texts can help us better understand our text.

The word *tachat* appears many times in Scripture, always meaning "in place of," or "on account of," and never "as identical substitution for."

Some examples:

"And if he cause his servant's tooth or his maidservant's tooth to fall out, he shall let him go free *for* (*tachat*) his tooth's sake" (Exodus 21:27).

" . . . and Abraham went and took the ram and brought it up for a burnt offering *instead of* (*tachat*) his son" (Genesis 22:13).

"And the men said unto her: 'Our life *in place of* yours (*tachteichem*), if ye tell not this our business . . .' " (Joshua 2:14).

The meaning of this last quote is that if the enemy tries to kill Rahab and her family, then these men will fight to the death, if necessary, in order to save her life. They will give their lives in place of her giving hers. The meaning is certainly not that if she dies they, too, will give their lives (*tachteichem*).

Likewise, in the earlier examples cited, the meaning of the word *tachat* is "in place of," or "on account of," but not as identical substitution for the person or object in question. By noting the similar word *tachat* in other passages of the Scriptures and construing its meaning there, we are led to a more accurate understanding of its meaning in our text.

Logic, the text and our Key to Interpretation all lead to the same conclusion: an eye for an eye means *to give* something *in place of* the lost eye, that being monetary compensation.

Example 4—"To Give the Younger before the Firstborn"

Word associations across texts can also be a most exquisite vehicle for conveying subtle moral messages in the Torah. After Laban had promised to give his daughter Rachel to Jacob in marriage, he tricked Jacob, and gave him Leah instead.

> And it came to pass, that in the morning, behold it was Leah: and he said to Laban, What is this that you have done to me? Did I not serve with you for Rachel? wherefore then have you deceived me? And Laban said, It is not done so in our place, to give *the younger before the firstborn*. (Genesis 29:25–26)

Laban's phrase "the younger before the firstborn" is strange. The opposite of "younger" is "older," not "firstborn." As we find earlier in the chapter, "And Laban had two daughters; the name of the *elder* was Leah, and the name of the *younger* was Rachel" (Genesis 29:16).

But, as the commentator, Eliezer Askenazi (d. 1567), points out, Laban chose his words with biting sarcasm. Jacob had just fled his home after having deceived his father and stolen the firstborn's blessings intended for his brother Esau, the actual firstborn.

We can sense Laban's gloating tone as he relishes deceiving the deceiver, Jacob. He turns the knife in the open wound as he pontificates, "It is not done so in *our* place, to give the younger before the *firstborn!*"

Jacob has gotten his just deserts. And we are informed of the divine justice by Laban's clever word association.

The other side of the interpretive coin is noting differences between similar texts. Let us see what we can learn from this Key to Torah interpretation.

6

Key 4—Differences between Similar Texts

Unexpected inconsistencies in the Torah can be as revealing as are subtle similarities. Often we find an event or statement repeated twice in the Torah yet, while the details are basically the same, there are glaring differences between the two accounts.

These ostensible discrepancies cry out for interpretation. Too often academic biblical scholars consider them to be evidence of several oral traditions, "editorial oversights," inadvertent inconsistencies, signifying nothing. Glossing over inconsistencies in this way reflects a gross underestimation of the Torah's narrative precision and its literary sophistication. It also deprives one of retrieving valuable insights that the Torah intended to convey.

Actually, the classical Torah commentators differ among themselves in their approach to such differences between similar texts. Two main camps can be delineated. Those, like Ibn Ezra and David Kimchi, who usually view these phenomena as unremarkable expressions of the Torah's literary style. In such cases, there is neither need nor reason for further interpretation. Ibn Ezra, in his comment on the discrepancies between the two accounts of the Ten Tablets (in Exodus and later in Deuteronomy), makes this abundantly clear.

> Know that the words are like the body and the meaning is like the soul, so that a word is only the vessel for the meaning. [Therefore we] do not question a change in the wording as long as the meaning is the same.

This view is not shared by most rabbinic commentators. The Ramban and Rashi stand out as the noted exemplars of the opposing position: that nuances are not for naught and that there is both rhyme and reason to them. The following examples will, I hope, lend credence to the latter position. It should give the student impetus to explore the meaning of unexpected differences when he finds them in the Torah text.

Example 1—The Reason for *Shabbat*

The Ten Commandments (Decalogue) given at Sinai is recorded in two places in the Torah, one in Exodus (20:1–14) and again in Deuteronomy (5:6–18). The commentators have pondered the reasons for the various discrepancies between these two versions. We will look at one of the most noteworthy, that is, the two variant reasons given for the *Shabbat*.

In Exodus, we read:

> Remember the Sabbath day to sanctify it. Six days may thou labor and do all thy work. But the sev-

enth day is the Sabbath of the Lord your God, thou shall not do any work, thou, nor thy son, nor thy daughter, thy maidservant, nor thy beasts, nor thy stranger in thy gates. *For in six days the Lord made heaven and earth, the sea, and all that is in them, and rested on the seventh day: therefore the Lord blessed the Sabbath day and sanctified it.* (Exodus 20:8–11)

While, in Deuteronomy, a different reason is given for keeping the Sabbath:

Keep the Sabbath day to sanctify it, as the Lord your God has commanded you. Six days thou may labor and do all thy work. But on the seventh day is the Sabbath of the Lord your God: thou shalt not do any work, thou, nor thy son, nor thy daughter, thy servant, nor thy maidservant, nor any of thy herd, nor thy ass, nor thy beasts, nor thy stranger in thy gates; that thy manservant and thy maidservant may rest as well as thou. *And remember that thou were a servant in the land of Egypt, and that the Lord thy God brought thee out of there through a mighty hand and by a stretched out arm: therefore the Lord thy God commanded thee to keep the Sabbath day.* (Deuteronomy 5:12–15)

Here we have two different reasons given for the Sabbath as a day of rest. This glaring contradiction has puzzled commentators. But a careful reading of the text will eliminate the difficulty as if by magic. Compare the last sentences of both sections:

In Exodus, we read: "Therefore the Lord blessed the Sabbath day and sanctified it."

In Deuteronomy, we read: "Therefore the Lord thy God commanded thee to keep the Sabbath day."

In Exodus, we are told why the Sabbath is a special day, why the Lord blessed it: it was blessed because it was the culmination of the Creation. In Deuteronomy, the emphasis is different. We are told why, of all nations, the Jews are commanded to observe the Sabbath. It is not, after all, a national holiday—like Passover, for example, which is uniquely Jewish. The reason given in Deuteronomy is that since the Jews were slaves in Egypt and the Lord redeemed them, they are thus beholden to Him. They are commanded to proclaim His dominion in the world by keeping the Sabbath.

The discrepancy disappears once we look closely at the full text in the Torah.

Narrative portions of the Torah are replete with illuminating examples of differences between similar texts. These frequently are expressions of the tendentious intent of the individuals involved.

Example 2—A Wife for Isaac—Differing Reports

The story of Abraham's servant in search of a wife for his master's son Isaac (Genesis, chapter 24) is a story thrice told. In one of the longest chapters in the Torah, we read of Abraham committing his servant by oath to go to his homeland to find a wife for his son; we are then told of the servant's litmus test to choose the right girl ("the damsel that . . . shall say: Drink and I will give thy camels drink also . . ."), and how he found Rebecca. Later, the tale is told again from beginning to end as the servant recounts it to Rebecca's family. In the telling and the retelling, there are several significant discrepancies. Before you go further, I suggest you read the whole of chapter 24 first and see which ones you can find.

The Malbim dissects the chapter and notes many discrepancies. Following are several of them:

(1) Abraham Tells His Servant

Thou shalt not take a wife for my son of the daughters of Canaanites, among whom I dwell. But thou shalt go to *my country and to my kindred* and take a wife for my son Isaac. (Genesis 24:3–4).

(1a) Servant's Report to Laban

Thou shalt not take a wife for my son of the daughters of Canaanites, in whose land I dwell. But thou shalt go to *my father's house and to my family* and take a wife for my son. (Genesis 24:37–38)

While Abraham didn't limit taking a bride from his family only, the servant made the point to Rebecca's brother, Laban, as if it were his master's explicit request. We'll see the significance of this later.

The servant devised a diagnostic test to identify the girl fitting for Isaac.

(2) Servant's Prayer

"And it will be that the damsel to whom I shall say, Incline thy pitcher, I pray thee, that I may drink; and she shall say:

Drink and I will give thy camels drink also; let the same
be she that Thou hast appointed for Thy servant Isaac . . .'' (Genesis 24:14–15).

He is looking for a girl that will carry on Abraham's
tradition of kindness to strangers. The damsel's willing-
ness to put herself out, above and beyond that called for, is
his litmus test.

Now let us see what actually happened and what was
recounted to Laban and the family:

(3) What Happened	(3a) Servant's Report to Laban
And she said: *Drink my lord:* and she hastened and let down her pitcher upon her hand and gave him drink. *And when she had finished giving him drink, she said, I will draw water for thy camels also, until they have finished drinking.* (Genesis 24:18–19)	And she made haste and let down her pitcher from her shoulder and said: *Drink and I will give thy camels drink also.* (Genesis 24: 46–47)

The servant didn't tell it as it was. In actuality, Rebecca's
response wasn't precisely in accord with the servant's
conditions, as she first promised to give him drink and
only after she finished giving him to drink did she offer
to give drink for the camels. She seemed to follow the
talmudic advice of "say little but do a lot." The servant wasn't deterred by this deviation from his anticipated conditions, but the family would certainly be impressed by his clairvoyance if matters turned out exactly
as he predicted.

Before an interpretation of these differences is suggested, let's see one more:

(4) What Happened	(4a) Servant's Report to Laban
"And it came to pass as the camels had finished drinking that *the man took a golden pendant . . . and two bracelets for her hands . . . And he said: Whose daughter art thou? . . .*" (Genesis 24:22–23).	"*And I asked her and said: Whose daughter art thou?* And she said, The daughter of Bethuel, Nahor's son . . . *and I put the pendant on her nose and the bracelets on her hands*" (Genesis 24:47).

Again, the servant twisted matters in his retelling. While, in fact, he had given Rebecca the jewelry even before he knew she was of Abraham's family, that's not what he told Laban. He portrayed the events as if only after he knew she was of his master's family did he give her the gifts.

What can be made of all this? Or, we might ask of the servant's convenient memory lapses, is there method to his mendacity?

To consider these differences as insignificant deviations would be to miss an important theme that runs through this story. To understand the servant's clever editing of events we have to consider the ambiance of Abraham's country and his hierarchy of values.

Why does Abraham reject the Canaanite women and yet willingly accept a daughter-in-law from Laban's country, Padan-aram? Both were pagan societies, both were antithetical to Abraham's monotheistic beliefs.

The explanation is that the pagan society of Canaan was both perverse and corrupt. Sexual perversity was the norm and satanic theology the ideal. Padan-aram was no more sophisticated theologically than Canaan but their culture had reasonable social norms which held it together. Abraham, the father of ethical monotheism, cared less about people's beliefs than about their behavior, less about concepts than about precepts.

Abraham's servant devised an ethical test for choosing a bride, for he understood that character counted for more than devotion to religious catechisms. He also realized that Laban's society was one that was awed by witchcraft and wizardry, impressed by superstition and celestial signs. When talking to them he had to speak their language, relate to where they were coming from conceptually.

As we look at the servant's report to Laban and how he consistently deviates from what actually happened, we see how each deviation serves this purpose. By giving the impression that Abraham explicitly singled out Laban's family, which he did not (compare 1 and 1a above); by making it seem that the servant's silent prayer was answered exactly as prescribed, which it wasn't (compare 2 with 3 and 3a above); and by showing that he was more interested in Rebecca's family lineage than in her behavior, which he wasn't (compare 4 and 4a above), he gave a magical aura to the fulfillment of his prayer and thus transformed the natural chain of events into an uncanny celestial sign. In short, he boggled their magical mind-set. What do Laban and his reticent father say after hearing all these amazing details?

"Then Laban and Bethuel answered and said, The matter has gone forth from the Eternal: we cannot speak unto thee evil or good. Behold, Rebecca is before thee, take her, and go . . ." (Genesis 24:50–51).

Abraham would have been proud of his man in Padan-aram. The event was well-staged, perfectly directed, and superbly enacted. The proof was in the product. The pagans saw the hand of the Eternal.

The Differences between the Similar Texts made all the difference.

A similar analysis can—and should—be made on the deal struck between the sons of Jacob and the people of Shechem (Genesis, chapter 34).

The above example is typical, and not at all unusual, of the biblical narrative. Retelling is a special art in the Torah. The concise biblical style is ordinarily characterized by such summary statements as ''And they did so,'' or ''And they said to him the word's of Balak,'' or ''And he told Laban all of these things.'' Thus, whenever the Torah records a detailed retelling, we can take it as a rule that the retelling contains significant differences from the Torah's original report.

The story of Joseph and Potiphar's wife (Genesis, chapter 39) is a striking example of this. Z. Sorotzkin, in his commentary *Oznaim LaTorah,* compares several fine points of discrepancy in the telling and retelling of this story. Potiphar's wife tells the story of her alleged seduction by Joseph to two different audiences, with transparently tendentious intentions.

Example 3—Joseph and Potiphar's Wife

Joseph, sold into slavery, was bought by Potiphar, one of Pharaoh's ministers. Potiphar's wife took a liking to him and one day, when the two of them were alone, she made an unabashed advance. ''And it came to pass on such a day that Joseph went into the house to do his work, and there

was none of the men of the house there within. And she
caught him by the garment, saying, Lie with me; and he
left his garment in her hand and ran away, and went
outside" (Genesis 39:11–12).

Thus spurned and left awkwardly holding Joseph's garment, she deftly developed her alibi and revenge. She first
told her other servants, then later retold the events to her
husband. Here are the two versions. Note the differences
between them:

As Told to the Servants

And she called to the men
of her house, and spoke
unto them saying, See, he
has brought in a Hebrew
man to us to mock *us;* he
came unto me to lie with
me, and I called with a loud
voice. And it came to pass,
when he heard that I lifted
up my voice and called, that
he left his garment with
me, and ran away, and went
out. (Genesis 39:14–15).

As Told to Her Husband

And she placed his garment
by her, until his lord came
into his house. And she
spoke unto him according
to these words, saying, The
Hebrew *slave,* whom you
brought to us, came unto
me to mock *me.* And it came
to pass, as I lifted up my
voice and called, that he
left his garment with me,
and ran outside. (Genesis
39:16–18).

Note the slight but meaningful differences in these re-
ports. To the other workers (who were also slaves), she
refers to Joseph as a Hebrew "man," so as not alienate
them; to her husband, she made a point of calling him a
slave. To enlist the support of the other workers, she
identifies with them as she accuses her husband—"he has
brought a Hebrew man to mock *us.*" To him, she is more
specific—"The Hebrew slave you brought to us, came

unto me to mock *me.*'' Another subtle shift of emphasis in the biblical Hebrew transforms a clear insinuation of her husband's malicious intent into an ambiguous accusation. When she speaks to the other servants, she says, ''he brought to mock us,'' but when she tells her husband, she dampens and blurs her anger and says only, ''whom you brought to us, came unto me to mock me.''

The Torah forgoes its customary narrative shorthand in retelling events in order to give us added insight into the subjective perceptions and machinations of its characters. Yet these insights, too, are conveyed with skillful economy.

Detecting the differences between texts is the first step, making sense out of them the next. No entry into the deeper meaning of these texts can be made until we recognize the purposefulness of such seemingly erratic inconsistencies.

7

Key 5—Repetitions and Redundancies

Repetitions and Redundancies are grist for the mill of classical biblical exegesis. Understanding the purpose of seemingly gratuitous Repetitions and apparent Redundancies is one of the most frequently used interpretive Keys of both the early midrashic Sages and the medieval Torah commentators.

Given the basic assumption, one shared by all classical Torah commentators, that the Scripture is the faithful record of the Divine word, there was no latitude for unnecessary verbiage in the record. The midrashic and talmudic scholars, as well, derived many interpretive and halachic (legal) conclusions from "extra words" and, not infrequently, even extra letters in the text.

The Torah, in both its narrative portions as well as its halachic portions, is characteristically succinct. The famous story of the murder of Abel by his brother Cain is related in a mere twelve sentences and that includes Cain's punishment and his protection by means of the mark of Cain. Esau selling his birthright to Jacob for a pot of pottage is condensed into six pithy sentences. Brevity is the hallmark of Torah discourse. This is true for both the narrative and legal sections in the Torah.

In light of its telegraphic style, Repetitions and Redundancies stand out all the more starkly in the Scriptural text. The traditional Torah commentators, cognizant of the verbal precision of the Torah text, have centered in on these aberrations and foraged from them additional insights into the deeper meaning of the text.

In the examples that follow, I differentiate between cases of verbatim, or near verbatim, repetitions of previously stated material and those instances when the Torah text is seemingly redundant, that is, it restates in different words what has already been said. For our purposes, there is no essential difference between these two types; both appear to be superfluous and therefore demand interpretation. In both cases, a helpful interpretation will show us how the repeated or the redundant phrase enhances our understanding.

Nevertheless, perhaps we can discern that these two types—Repetitions and Redundancies—serve slightly different ends. We often find that repetitions serve the purpose of dramatizing a point, while redundancies are used to add a new dimension to our perception of the text.

Some repetitions are quite glaring and puzzling. For example, the sacrificial offerings brought by each tribe at the dedication of the Tabernacle (Numbers, chapter 7). Here, each prince of the twelve tribes brought the exact same combination of offerings; the Torah repeats the same formula for each tribe, with only the name of the prince being changed. This has caused much speculation among the commentators as to the reason for this repetition.

Every verbatim repetition demands an explanation. Some instances may be relatively easy to interpret. Others may prove recalcitrant to our best efforts. But our failure to reasonably interpret these repetitions does not invalidate our puzzlement. Questions remain questions regardless of our interpretive ability to unlock them. Unanswered questions are a most effective goad to further study and deeper understanding.

Let us look at several examples of this Key to understanding. While I offer just a select few, a sensitive ear can discern innumerable examples throughout the Torah.

Example 1—"And the Two of Them Went Together"

The drama of the Binding of Isaac is portrayed most powerfully by the Torah's subdued, minimalistic description of Abraham's ultimate test of faith.

After Abraham received the Divine command to bring his son, Isaac, up as a sacrificial offering to God, he traveled three days with his son and two lads. No conversation was recorded between them during those three days. Then Abraham and Isaac alone made their way up the mountain.

> And Abraham took the wood of the burnt offering and put it upon Isaac his son; and he took the fire in his hand and the slaughtering knife; *and they went both of them together.* And Isaac said unto Abraham his father, and he said: My father. And he said, Here I am, my son. And he said, Behold the fire and the wood but where is the sheep for a burnt offering? And Abraham said, My son, God will provide himself

the sheep for the burnt offering; *and they went both of them together.* (Genesis 22:6–8)

Here we have a fine example of the Torah's masterly use of repetition. These three sentences comprise a dynamically moving expression of what is, at once, an emphatic, dramatic, and thematic presentation. Emphatic, because the identical phrase is repeated twice within the space of three sentences. Even a casual reading will pick it up; the emphasis cannot escape the eye.

The drama is expressed as the repetition of the phrase "they went both of them together" explodes in our mind with a powerful insight—that the Isaac who now walks together with his father is not the same Isaac who walked a few moments earlier together with his father. The flickering doubt in Isaac's mind that something important is missing ("where is the sheep?") is transformed, by Abraham's cryptic answer, into the awesome certainty that he, in fact, is to be the offering. Now possessing this shattering awareness, Isaac, nevertheless, continues with the same innocence as before—"and they went both of them together."

We can see the two of them trudging up the mountain in dedicated determination, we can sense the emotional weight shared now by both of them, and we can hear the deafening silence as "they went both of them together."

The thematic dimension is driven home by means of the dramatic phrasing. We learn the significance of this act for both Abraham and Isaac. Not just Abraham was being tried; and not just Abraham stood up to this terrifying test of faith. Isaac, too, endured the test. He was not some blind object, waiting passively and impassively for Abraham to fulfill his commitment to God. The repetition has the force of telling us that Isaac was the willing, silent partner whose filial obedience and religious commitment were not shaken by the riveting realization of the unspeakable end that stood in store for him.

Look again, a closer look, at these sentences and we can discern another repetition here that carries its own message:

> *And Isaac said* unto Abraham his father, *and he said,* My father: and he said, Here I am, my son. *And he said,* Behold the fire and the wood but where is the sheep for a burnt offering? (Genesis 22:7)

Why is the phrase "and he said" repeated? The first phrase, "And Isaac said," does not introduce any statement by Isaac. We must wait for the second "and he said" before Isaac can clear his throat and speak up.

The repetition conveys hesitancy. Isaac begins to ask the question that is disturbing him, but he pauses. He can't get the words out. Perhaps he has a premonition of what the answer will be. He begins again, "and he said," but even now he can utter only one word (in Hebrew), "My father." Finally, he gets up the courage to express his foreboding doubts. Three times Isaac "says" but only twice does he speak! This reinforces our impression that even from the beginning Isaac was already dimly aware of the true purpose of this trip.

Redundancies present us with a similar interpretive problem as do repetitions. Our question in such cases is: Why restate, albeit in different words, what is already known? Interpretation here is the search for the additional message contained in the seemingly redundant phrase. Notice the following.

Example 2—"And Sarai Was Barren; She Had No Child" (Genesis 11:30).

If Sarai was barren, then by definition she had no child! The last phrase is totally redundant. If, on the other hand, the Torah would have described Sarai's situation in this way: "And Sarai had no child, she was barren," the second half of the sentence would have added to our understanding. Sarai had no child *because* she was barren, and not, for example, because she had lost a child at an early age. But to say that she was barren and then to say that "she had no child" is a transparent tautology.

The eleventh-century commentator Hizkuni suggests that the Torah is telling us that Sarai was barren and had no children at this time, whereas later she would be barren and nevertheless have a child! Meaning that her giving birth would be a true miracle—she would have a child yet even then she would remain biologically barren! In the language of the tabloids, "Barren woman gives birth!" The additional words alert us to the supernatural significance of the birth. In the words of the Talmud, "He who told the oil to burn could likewise tell the vinegar to burn." He who enables the miracle of normal childbirth to happen can likewise, in an equally miraculous way, enable barren women to give birth.

Some redundancies are not as noticeable.

Example 3—Joseph Dreams Again

When Joseph dreamt his dreams of future greatness, after his first dream we are told: "And he dreamed again another dream" (Genesis 37:9). The words "again" and "another" seem to be redundant, since using any one of them alone would convey the same meaning.

"And he dreamed another dream."
"And he dreamed again a dream."

It would seem that both of these sentences have the same meaning. But a sensitive ear makes us aware of the fine distinction between them. The first sentence means that Joseph dreamt another—unrelated—dream, while the second sentence implies that he dreamt a repetition of the first dream. In fact, Joseph dreamt two dreams (one, of the sheaves bowing down to him; and one of the sun, moon and stars bowing down to him). Their manifest content was different, while their latent message was similar—Joseph's future superiority over his brothers. In essence, they were really one dream. The Torah conveys the inner tension of the contradiction—two dreams that were one—by telling us, "He dreamed again (similar) another (different) dream."

Biblical poetry and oration are replete with parallelisms, that is, verses constructed of two (or more) parts where the first half conveys the same idea as the second but in different words. To choose one of hundreds:

The ox knoweth his owner,
And the ass his master's crib;
But Israel doth not know,
My people doth not consider.
(Isaiah 1:3)

The sentence is made up of two halves; each half has the same idea repeated twice.

Or again from the Torah:

Give ear ye heavens,
and I will speak;
And let the earth hear
the words of my mouth.
    (Deuteronomy 32:1)

These parallelisms can be viewed as a poetic technique
for emphasizing a point. And some Torah commentators
see it this way. But others cannot accept the idea of strict
synonymity. Different words have different meanings,
however close they seem to be to one another. The interpreter's task is to listen attentively to each verbal nuance
to discover the additional messages being communicated.

Example 4—The Unique Sinaic Experience

*"Hath there been any thing as great as this, or hath
there ever been heard like it?"* (Deuteronomy 4:32)

Moses, in his long farewell speech to the people, selec-
tively reviewed Jewish history to impress upon the younger generation their obligation to carry on the Covenant
of the Forefathers. The words quoted above refer to
the momentous and unique Sinaic Revelation. We have a
case of parallelism here: Has there been . . . ? Has there
been heard . . . ?

What might the redundancy mean here? We quote further to give a fuller picture.

Did ever a people hear the voice of God speaking out of the midst of the fire, as thou hast heard and live? . . . Out of heaven He made thee to hear His voice, that He might instruct thee, and upon earth He shewed thee His great fire; and thou heardest His words out of the midst of the fire. (Deuteronomy 4:33–36)

Moses is saying that never before in history had a whole people, some six hundred thousand adult males, experienced a communal Divine Revelation. Individuals experiencing prophetic revelation have been recorded by many nations in the societies of ancient times. Individual aberrations are always possible and continue to be reported even up to the present day. But revelation *en masse* had no parallel in the ancient world. "Has there ever been a thing as great as this?"

The startling thing is Moses' next statement: "Hath there ever been heard . . . ?" The difference between "has there been" and "has there been heard" is that, even if there had never been such an event as a nationwide revelation, it is still possible that such an oral tradition existed in a people's folklore and they had, in fact, "heard of it." This would be a myth which was passed on from generation to generation and accepted as history, as a part of one's heritage. Certainly, thousands witnessing and personally participating in a dramatic spiritual revelation is not the kind of testimony that can be summarily brushed off. Such a claim, if it could be passed off as true, would give a people's faith added validity. This kind of oral tradition would be a case of "it having been heard" even though it "never really had been."

What Moses may be claiming, in his parallel phrasing, is that no people has ever experienced a mass Revelation such as did the Jews at Sinai, nor have any *even invented such a story*—presumably, it being too difficult to pass off as history.

Moses' statement, made over 3,000 years ago, retains its validity to the present day since, in fact, no cult or religion has ever made such a sweeping claim, except the Jews in their Bible!

Interpreting our text in this way gives it a prophetic flavor. This may make the rationalist student more than a little queasy. But the interpretation must be judged on its own merits as to whether it adequately explains the text. The homiletics are open to those who choose to use them.

Occasionally, we will find the narrator's repetition concealing and revealing at the same time. I have already focused on the request of the tribes of Gad and Reuben in chapter 3. But within that story, we find an interesting repetition that is easily overlooked.

Example 5—The Pregnant Pause

The children of Gad and the children of Reuben came and *said* to Moses and to Elazar the priest and to the princes of the congregation, saying: Ataroth, and Dibon, and Jazar, and Nimrah, and Heshbom, and Elealah, and Sebam, and Nebo, and Beon. The country which the Eternal smote before the congregation of Israel is a land of cattle and thy servants have cattle. *And they said:* if we have found favor in thine eyes, let this land be given to thy servants for a possession, and make us not pass over the Jordan. (Numbers 32:2–5)

The text has "and said," and again, "and they said," with no one else speaking in between. The repetition is telling. There is no need for the second "And they said." It has the force of the start of new conversation.

We hear the tribes making their case by stating the already-known facts: "the country which the Eternal smote . . . is a land of cattle . . . and thy servants have cattle. . . ."

And they pause. They wait for Moses to draw the obvious conclusion and offer them the Transjordan on his own. They don't want to grovel; they wait for Moses to follow their ineluctable logic, "a land of cattle . . . your servants have cattle. . . ." They wait and wait, but Moses says not a word. We can see the tribes' spokesmen getting fidgety, shifting from foot to foot, looking at each other in puzzled dismay as Moses waits in silence.

But Moses was on to their tricks. He waited patiently for the other shoe to fall. He made them sweat it out, he gave nothing away. When the tribesmen saw their planned scenario failing, they pulled back from their assertive silence and began again, reluctantly, forced to spell out, and spill out, the obvious. In reticent entreaty, they open their plea again: "*And they said:* If we have found favor in thine eyes, let this land be given to thy servants for a possession. . . ."

By this time, it is redundant to repeat that redundancies in the Torah-text are never simply repetitions, nor are repetitions merely redundancies. They exist to tell us something. The work of interpretation is to figure out what that something is.

8

Key 6—Word Order

One of the most obvious, and at the same time, most subtle, means by which we communicate nuances in meaning is by the way we choose to order our words. In ordinary conversation, we organize our sentences with an unconscious sensitivity to the different implications inherent in word order. When we listen to others, we intuitively recognize the different nuances of varied word sequences. The significance of word order is also apparent in the Torah's skillful use of literary allusion. An analysis of the Torah's language reveals an exquisitely sensitive use of Word Order to convey intended emphasis. By training our ear to notice these subtleties, we become conscious of the omnipresence of the phenomenon and become attuned to deeper messages in the text.

As an example from ordinary conversation, the following sentences contain the same words but, because of changes in their order, they convey different meanings. Note the difference in emphasis between them:

1. He went down.
2. Down he went.

The first sentence is clear enough; it tells us that someone went down. The second sentence, on the other hand, conveys quite a bit more. We get the impression that the fellow slipped or fell suddenly. There's an element of surprise here. Why do the same three words, when ordered differently, convey different meanings? By placing the word "down" first in the sentence, we give it special emphasis. "Down" is what happened. And it happened immediately. Whereas, in the first sentence, the word "went" comes before "down," telling us that the main point is that he went somewhere. Where he went and how he went are secondary.

In chapter 3, we discussed the story of the tribes of Reuben and Gad. There we saw how the Torah, by a choice of word order, brought home the message that they valued their possessions more than themselves and their families. The phrasing in the Torah placed their possessions ("much cattle") before themselves ("the children of Gad and the children of Reuben"). The Word Order pointedly imparted a moral of great substance.

Example 1—Inspiration and David's Psalms

The Sages of the Talmud were sensitive to the implications of Word Order. They noted that in the Book of Psalms the introductory titles of the psalms have special significance. Among them, we find, for example:

A psalm to David. The Lord is my shepherd, I shall not want. In lush meadows He lays me down, beside tranquil waters He leads me. . . . (Psalm 23)

While in the very next psalm we find:

To David a psalm. To the Lord is the earth and the fullness thereof, the inhabited land and those who dwell in it. . . . (Psalm 24)

The lead captions of the two psalms are reversed; one begins with "A psalm to David," while the next begins with "To David a psalm." Is there any significance in this reversal?

The talmudic Sages suggest an unusual interpretation (*Pesachim* 117a). They explain that, whenever a psalm is introduced with the words "To David a psalm," the implication is that David first received Divine inspiration and only then proceeded to compose his psalm. On the other hand, when the caption reads "A psalm to David," this tells us that first David began to compose and only later did the inspiration come upon him. This gives us a revealing insight into the complexity of the creation of David's classic work. The Sages' interpretation gives us a feel for the interactive influences of personal creative genius and Divine inspiration in David's psalms.

This interpretation also tells us something about the workings of Word Order. We can conclude that the first word of the phrase is the decisive one. Thus, when the word "David" comes first, David's inspiration came first; when the word "psalm" comes first, the (writing of the) psalm came first, even before his inspiration.

Thus we can conclude that the order of words determines emphasis. And when we have Word Order reversals, the former word is meant to carry the emphasis.

Example 2—Announcing the Birth of Isaac

This is strikingly illustrated in the story of the angels who visited Abraham and Sarah to inform them that Sarah will bear a son:

> And he said: I will certainly return unto thee when the season comes around; and, behold, *a son will [be born] to Sarah* your wife. And Sarah heard in the tent door, which was behind him, Now Abraham and Sarah were old and well stricken in age; it had ceased to be with Sarah after the manner of women. And Sarah laughed within herself, saying: "After I am waxed old shall I have pleasure, my lord being old also?" And the Lord said unto Abraham: 'Wherefore did Sarah laugh, saying: Shall I of a surety give birth, who am old? Is anything too hard for the Lord? At the set time I will return unto thee, when the season comes around, and *to Sarah [will be born] a son.* (Genesis 18:10-14)

Note that the first time it says "a son to Sarah," and later, "to Sarah a son." The reason for this deliberate reversal can be gleaned from the context, as Yaakov Meklenberg (1785–1865) has pointed out. We understand that the first time the message is delivered the point of the tidings is to tell Abraham that a son would be born to him ("a son will be born . . ."). When Sarah couldn't believe that at her age she could bear a son, the angel then emphasized that indeed *Sarah* will give birth and thus "To Sarah [will be born] a son."

The presence of an interpretation-laden Word Order becomes apparent when the same words are repeated but with their order reversed, as in the cases above. These reversals are never without meaning. The midrashic Sages were keenly aware of the significance of the ordering of words and their reversal. Let's compare a midrashic interpretation with one that can be derived from our Plain Sense interpretation.

Example 3—"In the Midst of the Sea"

In Exodus 14, we are told of the crossing of the Reed Sea:

> And the children of Israel *came into the midst of the sea upon the dry land;* and the waters were a wall to them on their right, and on their left. (Exodus 14:22)

Compare this with the following sentence:

> And the children of Israel *walked upon dry land in the midst of the sea;* and the waters were a wall unto them on their right, and on their left. (Exodus 14:29)

In the first phrase, the children of Israel are initially reported to have come into the sea and then upon dry land. In the second, the words are reversed, that is, they first walked on the dry land and then into the midst of the sea. All the same, you say. Well, the Midrash thinks it's significant enough to comment on:

> If they came into the sea, how is it they were on dry land? And if they were on dry land why then "in the midst of the sea"? But from here we learn that the sea wasn't split for them until they came into the waters

up to their nostrils, then it became dry land. (*Exodus Rabbah* 21:10)

The message of the Midrash is clear. The crossing of the Reed Sea was a test of faith for the fleeing Israelites. Those who dared, threw themselves into the waters, placing their lives in the hands of the Almighty. Their total trust was rewarded by the miracle of the waters becoming dry land.

The less faithful and more fearful waited till a dry path was spread out before them and only then did they go "on the dry land in the midst of the sea."

This is a beautiful Midrash which graphically depicts the rewards of faith over fear. But how would a *P'shat* interpretation approach the changes in phrasing between the two texts?

By seeing the different contexts of each of the phrases, it should become clear why each phrasing was chosen. Let us look at the two sentences in their respective contexts.

And Moses stretched out his hand over the sea; and the Eternal caused the sea to go back by a powerful east wind all that night, and made the sea dry, and the waters were divided. And the children of Israel came into the midst of the sea upon the dry land; and the waters were a wall unto them on their right, and on their left. (Exodus 14:21–22)

Here the miracle is first described in all its wonder. The east wind cut a path in the midst of the sea and the Israelites went right through where the sea once was. Thus, we are told that they went "into the midst of the sea . . . ." The words are reversed (first dry land, then sea) in the following context:

> And Moses stretched forth his hand over the sea, and the sea returned to its continuity at the turning of the morning; and the Egyptians fled towards it; and the Eternal overthrew the Egyptians in the midst of the sea. And the waters returned, and covered the chariots, and the horsemen, and all the forces of Pharaoh that came into the sea after them; there remained not so much as one of them. But the children of Israel walked upon the dry land in the midst of the sea; and the waters were a wall unto them on their right, and on their left. (Exodus 14:27–29)

The emphasis here is clearly on the contrast between the plight of the ill-fated Egyptians as the sea swallowed them up and that of the Israelites as they "walked upon the dry land" in the midst of that very same sea that was drowning their enemies.

In each case, the Word Order reflects that aspect of the crossing of the Reed Sea that needs highlighting. The Word Order is a subdued way of drawing our attention to the salient parts of the Torah's message.

Example 4—Honoring/Fearing One's Parents

We find an interesting psychological insight conveyed by word reversal when the Torah teaches us about one's filial obligations toward one's parents.

Compare these two sentences:

"Honor your *father and your mother*" (Exodus 20:12).
"Every man, *his mother and his father* shall he fear"
(Leviticus 19:3).

Notice how the parental order is reversed in these
two commands. In the first command dealing with honoring one's parents, father comes before mother. In the
second, regarding fearing one's parents, mother comes
before father.

Is this a haphazard reversal? Hardly.

The Talmud makes the point that normally children
fear their father more than their mother. And, in order to
counteract this and stress the importance of fearing one's
mother as well, mother was placed first in this command.
On the other hand, when it comes to the warmer relationship of honoring one's parents, the child feels closer to his
mother and thus would naturally honor her more than he
would his more disciplining father. In this case, the Torah
stresses the need to honor one's father. This is done by
placing father before mother in the command.

The order in which words are arranged in the sentence
may convey more than emphasis; it may reflect the arrangement of reality.

Example 5—Separation of the Sexes in Noah's Ark

In Genesis 7:7, we read of Noah entering the Ark with his
family:

And Noah came in, and his sons, and his wife, and his
sons' wives with him, into the ark, because of the
waters of the deluge.

After the flood, they are commanded to leave the ark and return to normal life on earth:

And God spake unto Noah saying. Go out of the ark, thou, and thy wife, and thy sons, and thy sons' wives with thee. (Genesis 8:15–16)

Rashi makes us aware of the difference in Word Order between these two sentences. We note that, when the family entered the ark, the sexes were separated ("Noah and his sons . . . his wife, and his sons' wives"); whereas, when they left the ark after the flood, the husbands and wives were reunited ("thou and thy wife . . . thy sons, and thy sons' wives"). The difference is interpreted by Rashi to mean that during the flood, when the world was in a state of distress, sexual cohabitation was forbidden.

Conducting business as usual, including indulging in personal gratifications, would show a callous disregard for the suffering of the rest of mankind. Even though Noah was spared the flood's destruction, he and his family identified with the sorrow of the world and refrained from sexual contact with their wives. Only afterwards, when peace had returned to earth, were the few surviving men and women permitted to cohabit.

The order of words here clues us in to the family's behavior and its moral lesson.

I shouldn't give the impression that only when we find word reversals is Word Order worthy of interpretation. All Word Order is open to interpretation. In most cases, the meaning is sensed without analysis. But, occasionally, an important emphasis is conveyed in the Word Order, an emphasis not available to us from content analysis alone.

9

Key 7—The Psychological Dimension

One of the most fascinating aspects of the biblical record is its sensitivity to the psychological dimension in human affairs. This comes across both in the narrative portions of the Torah as well as in its legal (halachic) sections. A sagacious appreciation of the human condition in its manifold expressions is exhibited throughout the biblical literature. This is not to say that you will find psychological principles spelled out in the Torah as in some textbook. The psychological dimension insinuates itself into warp and woof of the text.

At times these psychological lessons appear quite openly as when the Torah commands "And thou shalt not oppress a stranger for you know the soul of the stranger, because you were strangers in the land of Egypt" (Exodus 23:9). The message is clearly that because of your own personal experience, you can identify psychologically with the stranger. This identification and empathy afford you a unique understanding of the stranger's suffering; thus you must refrain from causing him similar suffering.

Example 1—"Love Thy Neighbor as Thyself"

Sometimes the psychological message is conveyed in a less obvious manner—as in the familiar, though misunderstood, commandment to "love thy neighbor as thyself" (Leviticus 19:18). The saintly sounding injunction is uncharacteristic of the Bible's down-to-earth perspective of man and his frailties and limitations. To truly love another to the same extent one loves and cares for oneself is beyond the reach of most, if not all, men. The unlikelihood of achieving such a level of brotherly love would discourage a person from ever trying. How then are we to understand this pillar of ethical monotheism?

The Talmud records the story of the gentile asking Hillel the Elder to teach him the complete Torah while standing on one foot. Hillel's famous answer was "What is hateful to you, don't do to your neighbor. That is the whole Torah. The rest is commentary. Go and learn it." What he told the gentile was the obverse of the Golden Rule ("Love thy neighbor as thyself"), some say, because the negative is easier to master and sufficient for a beginner.

But what of the biblical command itself? How can it be reconciled as a reasonably achievable precept? A closer reading of the Hebrew text sets matters straight. The Hebrew reads *"V'ahavta l'reiacha kamocha."* This translates correctly to "Love *to* your neighbor as yourself" and not "Love your neighbor as yourself." This is as awkward in Hebrew as it is in English and requires explanation. The Ramban (d. 1270), one of the most psychologically attuned of the classical Torah commentators, interprets the grammatical peculiarity thus: "Do [acts of] love to your neighbor as you would have him do to you."

Looked at in this way its meaning is comprehensible. We are not enjoined to achieve some superhuman feat of emotional egalitarianism. Rather we are to behave in ways that are perceived by others as acts of love. Such a behavioral injunction is within a man's grasp. A sensitive psychological point has been made by the use of a fine grammatical twist.

We also saw, in the chapter on Word Order, the Torah's psychological awareness as it was expressed in the command to respect and honor one's parents.

Example 2—"Thou Shalt Not Hate Thy Brother in Thine Heart"

As we have seen, the Torah's realistic perception of the human condition and its awareness of man's psychological constraints excludes the possibility of legislating emotional adherence. It realizes that "the heart has its reasons that reason knows not" and thus we often have no direct or rational control over emotions.

Yet we do find an explicit and direct command forbidding an emotion. We are prohibited from hating one's fellowman "in one's heart." The sentence immediately preceding the Golden Rule says:

> Thou shalt not hate thy brother in thine heart; thou shalt certainly reprove thy companion and bear no sin on his account. (Leviticus 19:17)

This striking exception to the Torah's implicit rule of legislating behavior rather than emotions is baffling.

Present day psychological knowledge can shine light on this question. From family relations to international relations communication has rightly been hailed as the antidote to conflict. When nations talk with each other, we are told, they will not make war with each other. When individuals talk with each other, they are less likely to bear grudges against each other—good fences make good neighbors, notwithstanding. There is something about the human psyche that is repelled by the dissonance created when talking with someone we hate.

Psychologists have a name for it; their term is cognitive dissonance. When a person's outer behavior is not in accord with his inner feelings, dissonance and tension are created, and as a consequence, the need to resolve the dissonance and dissolve the tension.

Talking draws together, hatred tears apart. Thus if one perforce talks with an enemy with whom he would rather not talk, he is engaged in dissonant behavior—hating someone and yet talking with him. The psychological need to act in consonance with our feelings and to feel in line with our actions motivates us into aligning our feelings to coincide with our overt actions. In the case of talking with an enemy, this would be done by having the hatred dispelled; this extricates us from the psychological tension. We now feel (friendly) in concert with the way we act. In sum, talking with our enemy reduces our hatred toward him.

All this is wrapped up in our sentence. And while the command does, in fact, prohibit hatred in one's heart, it also immediately teaches us how to dispel that hatred. Reprove your neighbor, speak with him, communicate with him; in this way you can overcome your hatred and "bear no sin on his account."

That this, in fact, is the Torah's intent can be deduced from the text itself. Note that the advice to reprove one's neighbor is placed within the same sentence as the prohibition to hate him. This indicates that there is a causal relationship between the two parts of the sentence. Don't hate—reprove, talk and in so doing you will dissipate your hatred.

A modern psychological principle is unobtrusively tucked away in this corner of the Torah and incorporated into its code of conduct. This is a striking example of the Torah's psychological insight and its practical approach to the modification of human emotion. Twentieth-century man knows of no better way to accomplish this difficult task.

The psychological dimension also finds expression in the narrative portions of the Torah, sometimes in a most discerning way. That psychological threads can be uncovered in the text is all the more surprising when we realize how sparse are the Torah accounts of episodes. A superficial reading of the Torah would miss some of its most brilliant insights into human nature. Major personalities in the Torah are drawn in the most terse manner. Yet biblical personalities have a psychological consistency and coherence that ring true. Once a personage has been introduced in the Scripture we can usually discern the main lines of his personality behind his actions.

This too is as it is in life as we know it. Willingly or not, we reveal ourselves in all we do, try as we may to conceal our darker impulses. And as the observer must be psychologically keen to the nuances of human behavior in order to see below the surface of things, so too must the student of Torah be psychologically attuned to the nuances of the text to see the meanings below its surface.

Example 3—Saul's Self-Doubts

The first king of Israel, Saul the Benjamite, was appointed and anointed by Samuel. When Saul was chosen, he revealed his deep humility. He said: "Am I not a Benjamite, of the smallest of the tribes of Israel? and my family the least of all the families of the tribe of Benjamin? Wherefore then do you speak to me in this manner?" (1 Samuel 9:21). This character trait of ingenuous modesty, when inappropriately expressed, was to be Saul's undoing. His humility led him to follow the people and their wishes, instead of leading them (chap. 15).

This character trait acts as a crimson thread weaving its way through all of Saul's behavior, as we read in the First Book of Samuel. This is reflected in Samuel's famous rebuke of Saul when he took the Amalekite King Agag captive instead of killing him as commanded by God.

> Though thou be little in thine own sight, art thou not head of the tribes of Israel? (1 Samuel 15:17)

With this background let us examine another event in Saul's life and see how recognizing this personality trait enables us better to understand his behavior.

The text in question concerns Saul's battles with the Philistines. Prior to one of these battles, Saul sought counsel from God as to whether he should go to war or not. He received no answer from the Divine oracle and concluded that the Divine silence was due to some sin committed by the people. In order to determine who the sinner was, Saul devised a lottery to locate the guilty one. The people would be divided in two, then lots cast to see within which group the sinner was. By smaller and smaller subdivisions and the process of elimination, the culprit would eventually be caught.

Logic would dictate that the people be divided into two equal groups, so that 50 percent could be eliminated at the first pulling of lots, then divided again into two equal groups, so that 50 percent of that halved group would be eliminated and so on. What, in fact, did Saul do? As you examine the text below, look for the psychological dimension and how it finds expression.

> Then [Saul] said unto all Israel: Be ye [all the people] on one side and I and Jonathan my son will be on the other side. (1 Samuel 14:40)

This is certainly a strange way of going about a process of elimination. If the lots were to fall on the people's side only two people (Saul and Jonathan) will have been acquitted. The search would have to go on with the whole people, minus two.

What was driving Saul to make such a lopsided division and lottery? Clearly his behavior wasn't primarily motivated by a desire for the efficient apprehension of the sinner. His inner motivation seems to be first and foremost his need to prove his and his family's innocence! He assumed that with his son Jonathan and he standing alone they could be exonerated immediately; only then could Saul go about the business of finding the guilty one. (Ironically it was Jonathan who was the guilty one, located by the lottery for having unwittingly transgressed a decree of his father!)

Saul's inner doubts about his acceptance by man and God were the motive force behind his strange behavior. He was driven into the defensive position of proving his innocence when no one had even accused him! Appreciating the psychological dimension imbedded within the story affords us a deeper understanding of this story.

Example 4—Bilam's Lame Defense

In the story of Bilam, the pagan prophet, we find an interesting discrepancy which is easily overlooked. Balak, the king of Moab, hires Bilam the sorcerer/prophet to curse the Jews during their wanderings in the wilderness. King Balak sends messengers to convince Bilam to take on the job. He initially refuses. We read in Numbers 22:2:

> And Bilam answered and said unto the servants of Balak: If Balak would give me his house full of silver and gold, I cannot go beyond the word of the Lord my God, *to do a small or a big thing*.

Eventually Bilam is persuaded and he goes to curse the Jews in their encampment. Several attempts on his part all meet with failure and instead of cursing them he ends up blessing them. Balak, in a rage, vehemently castigates Bilam. In his defense Bilam answers:

> And Bilam said unto Balak. Did I not say to your messengers which you sent unto me saying. If Balak would give me his house full of silver and gold I cannot go beyond the word of the Lord, *to do either good or bad*. . . . (Numbers 24:12)

The discrepancy: Originally Bilam had said he could not do a "small or a big thing" beyond the word of God.

At the end of the story, Bilam, in his defense, quotes himself nearly word for word except for the end when he says he cannot do "either good or bad." The discrepancy in the quotes, when placed next to each other, is striking. But because the two sentences are separated by two full chapters we tend to pay no attention to it. Nevertheless, the discrepancy is blatant and demands an explanation.

With some thought we can understand Bilam's psychology and cunning. Initially Bilam, unsure of his ability to successfully curse the Jews, hedged his bet and explained his reluctance by saying he didn't know if his curse would accomplish anything, possibly not a lot and maybe not even a little.

His curses were unexpectedly transformed into blessings, and his "good intentions" (to curse) were turned on their head and he actually did harm to Balak (by blessing his enemies). It was at that point, after his embarrassing fiasco, that Bilam surreptitiously covered his tracks with the classic "I told you so." Had he not said, "I can't go beyond the word of the Lord to do good or bad"? In fact, he never said such a thing, but who would remember?

The fact that Bilam quotes himself verbatim, except for the crucial switch in words (from "small or big" to "good or bad"), is evident testimony that the difference between the two passages is not a fortuitous one. The words men choose to express themselves always reveal something about the inner workings of their personality. The Torah is a faithful recorder of conversations. Careful listening tunes us in to the psychological subtleties of the symphony of speech.

At times we may come across a passage in the Torah that doesn't sit right with our conception of human psychology.

It becomes a prod to questioning the meaning of the text. Such questions are legitimate and answers should be sought within the text. Following is an example of something that strikes us as an inappropriate emotional reaction on the part of Jacob.

Example 5—"They Were in His Eyes as But a Few Days . . ."

Jacob worked for his beloved Rachel for seven years.

> And Jacob worked seven years for Rachel and they were in his eyes as but a few days for the love he had to her. (Genesis 29:19)

They seemed as a few days because of his love for her? Just the opposite would seem normal. If he loved her and wanted her as his wife then seven years would seem like an eternity! Why did Jacob see things otherwise?

Attempts have been made to explain this puzzling text. But they either distort the text or strain our understanding of human psychology.

The answer, as Joseph Bekhor Shor (12th century) makes us aware, is in the Torah-text itself.

> And Laban said unto Jacob: Is it because you are my brother that you should serve me for nothing? Tell me what are your wages? . . . And Jacob loved Rachel and said: I will serve you seven years for Rachel your younger daughter. And Laban said: It is better that I give her to you than that I should give her to another man, abide with me. And Jacob served

seven years for Rachel and they were in his eyes as but
a few days. . . .

From here it is clear that it was Jacob who set the price of
seven years of labor for Rachel, and not Laban as we might
have assumed. To us the price may seem excessive, but it
was not so for Jacob. The price of seven years' labor was in
his eyes as but a few days because he loved Rachel so much
and thought she was worth so much more!

There is no reason to assume that human psychology
today is any different from human psychology in biblical
times. In fact it is precisely our ability to identify with the
human reactions of biblical figures that makes the moral
lessons of the Bible so much more telling. Our psychological instincts must be listened to when we study the Torah.
They can enhance our understanding in any one of a
number of ways. They may raise questions in our mind
about the text (like the case of Jacob's reaction); they may
deepen our understanding of the stories in the text (like
the case with Saul's strange behavior in throwing lots);
and they may expand and enrich our psychological understanding of human behavior (as in the laws of not
hating one's neighbor).

Living, as we do, in an era when the psychological
dimension dominates our evaluation of all things human,
this key to Torah understanding is all the more relevant. Our psychological enlightenment enables us to perceive the Torah's sophistication and wisdom in matters of
the soul.

10

Key 8—The Seven Code

An obscure feature of the Torah's composition is an intriguing aspect of its form rather than its content. The methods of Torah interpretation, which is the subject of this book, relate in one way or another to understanding the content of the text. But the Torah has its texture as well as its text.

The words and sentences that make up a text are organized in ways that convey their message in a most effective manner. But within this construction may be woven other patterns not adhering to the usual constraints of compositional convention. Such patterns are rare occurrences in prose literature; when they do occur, they may be considered ornamentations to the text and not essential to its message. An exception that comes to mind is a case where a message is coded within the text, the purpose being to avoid detection by the enemy. In that case, the manifest text is but a subterfuge while the code is the real message.

It will probably come as a surprise to many that the Bible, too, has its unique code. In addition to the Bible's poetic beauty, it contains a coded texture which in no way cramps its textual message or its literary power. I am referring to the curious phenomenon called the Seven Code, which is the repetition of identical words or phrases seven times (or multiples thereof) within a given section.

In all fairness, it must be said that including a discussion of the Seven Code in a book that deals with Plain Sense *(P'shat)* interpretation may seem somewhat inappropriate. The Seven Code is not *P'shat* in the conventional sense of the term. Nevertheless, I do consider it relevant to my thesis because the Seven Code pattern exists within the text itself and this is a critical criterion of Plain Sense interpretation. A second reason for including this code in a discussion of *P'shat* is that it too can serve as an aid in the work of interpretation.

The Seven Code is a relatively recent discovery in Torah interpretation. Its earliest mention was in a small booklet entitled *"Maftaiach HaYam,"* published in 1788 in Italy. The author, a blind scholar, points out many instances in the Torah where words are repeated in units of seven. The idea was picked up again in the beginning of this century when a German scholar by the name of Oskar Goldberg published articles on number patterns in the Torah, one of the more prominent ones being the seven pattern. Buber has also pointed out the significance of the *Leitwort*— "Lead word"—a word that is repeated often, which highlights the motif of a section. And while he has also alluded to seven-fold repetitions, his *Leitwort* is meant to include any number of word repetitions which is unusual. More recently, the late Professor Umanual Cassutto of Hebrew University, in his monumental work on Genesis and Exodus, also discusses the existence of a Seven Scheme in the Torah.

Cassutto points out, for example, that the first chapter of Genesis is replete with the Seven Code. The very first sentence, "In the beginning God created the Heavens and the Earth," has seven words and twenty-eight letters in the Hebrew. The central theme of the seven days of creation is that the sum total of the creation is "Good" ("And He saw that it was Good"). The word "Good" appears seven times in the chapter.

When we examine the evidence closely, we see that this is no sleight-of-hand phenomenon. What is significant for our purposes is not only the discovery of the existence of the Seven Code but its use as an auxiliary interpretive Key for understanding the messages of the Torah.

The talmudic Sages have pointed out that the number seven is "beloved." They enumerate various instances where seven plays a part in the Bible:

- Seven days of creation
- The Seventh day is Holy—the Sabbath
- Seven weeks after Passover is the Holiday of Shavuoth
- Every Seventh year is the Year of Release; the land lies fallow, and debts are annulled
- Seven times Seven years brings the Jubilee year
- The Seventh month of the year ushers in the "New Year," Rosh Hashana, the month in which Yom Kippur and Succoth are also celebrated
- The Seventh generation from Adam was Henoch, who was "Taken by God" because of his righteousness
- Moses was the Seventh generation after Abraham
- David, King of Israel, was the Seventh son of Ishai

This list could be expanded with other instances. What is surprising is that, in spite of the awareness of the significance of the number seven, neither the talmudic Sages nor the classical commentators mention the existence of the Seven Word Code in the Torah.

What Is the Seven Word Code?

In numerous passages throughout the Torah, we find that individual words or word combinations are repeated in patterns of seven or multiples of seven. This is done with an encompassing consistency and a fascinating ingenuity. The Seven Code can be found in every one of the five Books of Moses.

We have already seen some examples of this in the chapter on Opening Sentences. We saw how the words "before God" were repeated seven times to emphasize the priorities that Moses was teaching the children of Reuben and Gad. We also saw how, in a halachic section, the seven-fold repetition of different words emphasized different aspects of the same laws. Scores of similar patterns have already been uncovered. These patterns at times seem to reflect the central theme of a section while at other times their purpose seems more aesthetic.

In this chapter I will point out some unusual examples of the Seven Code. The first example below demonstrates the Seven Code as an aesthetic adornment while the second illustrates its use as a theme marker.

Example 1—The Tablets of the Covenant

The Torah recounts Moses receiving the Tablets of the Covenant in two separate places, once in Exodus 31:18–32:19 and a second time in Deuteronomy 9:9–17 and

10:1–5. In both books, we are told of Moses receiving the first Tablets and then, after the sin of the Golden Calf, when Moses broke the first set, we are told of his receiving the second Tablets. The word "Tablets" (*Luchot* in Hebrew) is repeated seven times, both in the report of the first Tablets, and then again seven times in the report of the second Tablets (Exodus, chapter 32). In Deuteronomy, chapter 9, we find the same Seven Code in the story of the Tablets—one seven-fold grouping in the report of the first Tablets and then again in the report of the second Tablets. This alone is a spectacular display of the Seven Code reaching across separate books of the Torah. But a closer look at the arrangement of the seven words itself demonstrates a clever pattern within a pattern.

In Exodus, we find the word Tablets repeated twice in one sentence. Then, after a break of fifteen sentences, the word is again repeated five times within a space of five sentences. Later, when the second Tablets are referred to, we find the word repeated five times in quick succession (within four sentences) and then, after a break of twenty-three sentences, the word Tablets appears twice more in two adjoining sentences. The pattern that emerges looks like this:

$$2 \ldots 5 \ldots 5 \ldots 2$$

Here, embedded in the story of the Ten Commandments (the Tablets of the Covenant), the Seven Code is preserved while, at the same time, a Ten Code is woven into it, as if to pay deference to the Ten Commandments!

The exceptional nature of these repetitions is borne out by the fact that the word "tablets" *(luchot)* appears only four other times throughout the whole Pentateuch.

Example 2—The Sons of Jacob—Filial Obligation

The sale of Joseph into slavery by his brothers, his rise to leadership in Egypt, and the eventual confrontation between him and his brothers twenty-two years later is certainly one of the most galvanizing tales in the whole Bible. Many Torah themes are woven throughout this gripping drama. (See chapter 12 for an in-depth analysis of one theme.) One aspect of this story is the brothers' relationship to their brother Joseph vis-à-vis their obligation to their father, Jacob. The Seven Code finds expression in this theme as well.

The story begins in Genesis, chapter 37, when we read about the sale of Joseph into slavery. There, the word "brother" appears twenty-one times (three times seven). The story comes to its dramatic climax some eight chapters later when Judah entreats Joseph to allow the younger Benjamin to return to his father, Jacob. In this section, the word "father" appears twenty-eight times (four times seven). The Seven pattern acts as bookends embracing the entire story from both ends, the embedded message being that one's concern and respect for one's father (twenty-eight) outweighs one's sibling obligations (twenty-one). This, of course, is the overt message as well.

Example 3—Isaac's Wells

That the use of the Seven Code is not done mechanically can be seen from the following example:

In Genesis 26:13–33, we are told of Isaac's land disputes with Abimelech. Isaac's men dig wells which are a source of conflict with Abimelech. When this section is read in

English, we find the word "dig" repeated eight times; but, in the original Hebrew, the word *VaYachperu* ("and they dug") and its variations occur exactly seven times. Also, in verse 25, we find the unusual word *VaYichru* ("and they dug"), instead of the word *VaVachperu,* which was used until now. This seems to be a purposeful choice of words in order to keep to the framework of seven by using a word that also means "to dig," yet without exceeding the seven quota of the code word *VaYachperu.*

A closer analysis will perhaps help us decipher the message behind this story. The nineteenth-century commentator Malbim points out that the two Hebrew words for dig, *chofer* and *koreh,* have slightly different meanings. *Koreh* means to start digging, while the word *chofer* means to complete a dig that had already been started. This subtle word variation indicates that Isaac's men re-dug previous wells, which usually led to conflict. After God appeared to Isaac (verse 24) and blessed him, his men *began digging* a well on their own *(VaYichru).* We can speculate that once Isaac received God's blessing, he, his men, and Abimelech all recognized Isaac's Divine right to the land. This was the last well dug; it led to a peace covenant between Isaac and Abimelech and it produced water!

The Seven Code was preserved in this story and a subtle message was conveyed by use of a non-code-word whose meaning was nearly, but not exactly, the same as the code-word.

The following example I offer with some hesitation. The reader may feel that I am stretching a point here, maybe even bending it out of shape! But I see it as an instance where the Seven Code is broken up and used to link together two separate, but related, stories.

Example 4—The Birthright: Sale and Delivery

The biblical story of Esau selling his birthright (Genesis
25:19–34) to his younger brother Jacob for a pot of porridge
is proverbial. Several chapters later (chapter 27), we read of
Isaac blessing Jacob, who had come in disguised as Esau:

> And the lads grew up; and Esau was a cunning hunter,
> a man of the field; but Jacob was a plain man, abiding
> in tents. And Isaac loved Esau, because he did eat of
> his venison; but Rebecca loves Jacob. And Jacob sod
> pottage; and Esau came from the field, and he was
> faint. And Esau said to Jacob, Let me devour, I pray
> thee, from this red, red thing, for I am faint: therefore
> his name is called Edom. And Jacob said, Sell me this
> day your *birthright*. And Esau said, Behold I am
> going to die; and what is this *birthright* to me? And
> Jacob said, Swear to me this day; and he swore to
> him; and he sold his *birthright* to Jacob. Then Jacob
> gave Esau bread and pottage of lentils, and he did eat
> and drink, and he rose, and went, and Esau despised
> the *birthright*. (Genesis 25:27–34)

The key word in chapter 25 is "birthright" or "firstborn" (both in Hebrew have the same root *bechor*) but it
appears only four times. When we cross over (chapters
and years) to the culmination of the birthright sale, when
Jacob comes to take the fruits of his earlier purchase as
Isaac blesses his son (chapter 27), we find the word "firstborn" (or birthright) again.

> . . . And he (Jacob) came to his father and said, My
> father; and he said, Here I am; who are you, my son?

And Jacob said to his father, I am Esau your *firstborn;*
I have done as you have spoken to me: arise, I pray
you, sit and eat of my venison, that your soul may
bless me. And Isaac said to his son, How is it that you
found it so quickly, my son? And he said, Because the
Lord God has caused it to happen before me. And
Isaac said to Jacob, Step near, I pray you, that I may
feel you, my son, whether you are my son Esau
himself or not. . . . And he stepped near, and kissed
him, and he smelled the odor of his garments, and
blessed him, and said, See, the odor of my son is as
the odor of a field which the Lord has blessed. . . .
And it came to pass, as soon as Isaac had finished
blessing Jacob, and Jacob was yet scarce gone out
from the face of Isaac his father, that Esau his brother
came in from his hunting. And he also made savory
meats, and brought them to his father, and said to his
father, Let my father rise and eat from his son's venison, that your soul may bless me. And Isaac his father
said to him, Who are you? And he said, I am your son,
the *firstborn,* Esau. And Isaac trembled with an exceedingly great trembling, and said, Who then is he
that has hunted venison and brought it to me, and I
have eaten of all before you came, and have blessed
him? Yea, and he shall be blessed. And when Esau
heard the words of his father, he cried with a great
and exceedingly bitter cry, and said to his father,
Bless me, even me also, O my father. And he said,
Your brother came subtly, and has taken your blessing. And he said, Is it because he was called Jacob that
he has supplanted me these two times? he took my
birthright and, behold, now he has taken my blessing. (Genesis 27:18–36)

Here the code word in Hebrew, *bechor,* is repeated three times.

The Seven Key clues us in to the connection between the two events: four plus three equals seven. Jacob receiving his father's blessing as a grown man is the ineluctable denouement of the childhood barter between the rash, impetuous Esau and the farsighted Jacob.

Example 5—Moses: Child and Man

The Seven Code is used skillfully as background music in the story of Moses. In the second chapter of Exodus, the Torah briefly recounts his birth and maturation into a responsible adult. Verses 1 through 22 constitute a complete section in the Torah. In the first half of this section (verses 1-10), we are told of the circumstances of Moses' birth and his being hidden and later discovered in his wicker cradle floating in the Nile. The second half of the section (verses 11-22) describes Moses' first encounter with the tribulations of his enslaved brothers in Egypt.

These two stories are deftly paralleled by the Seven Code.

A *man* went from the house of Levi and he took a daughter of Levi. The woman conceived and gave birth to a son. She saw that he was good and she hid him for three months. She could not hide him any longer, so she took for him a wicker basket and smeared it with clay and pitch; she placed the *child* into it and placed it among the reeds at the bank of the river. His sister stationed herself at a distance to know what would be done with him. Pharaoh's

daughter went down to bathe by the river and her
maidens walked along the river. She saw the basket
among the reeds and she sent her maidservant and she
took it. She opened it and saw him, the *child,* and,
behold, a youth was crying. She took pity on him and
said: This is one of the Hebrew children. His sister said
to Pharaoh's daughter: Shall I go and summon for you a
wet nurse from the Hebrew women, who will nurse
the *child* for you? The daughter of Pharaoh said: Go.
The girl went and summoned the *child's* mother. Pharaoh's daughter said to her: Take the *child* and nurse
him for me and I will give you your pay. So the woman
took the *child* and nursed him. The *child* grew up and
she brought him to the daughter of Pharaoh and he was
a son to her. And she called his name Moses, as she said:
For I drew him from the water. (Exodus 2:1–10)

The word *child* is repeated seven times. The story then
moves on to Moses' adult years:

It happened in those days that Moses grew up and went
out to his brothers and observed their burdens; and he
saw an Egyptian *man* strike a Hebrew *man,* of his
brothers. He turned this way and that and saw that
there was no *man,* so he struck down the Egyptian and
hid him in the sand. He went out the next day and behold! two Hebrew men were fighting. He said to the
wicked one: Why would you strike your fellow? He replied: Who appointed you as a dignitary, a ruler, and a
judge over us? Do you propose to murder me as you
murdered the Egyptian? Moses was frightened and he
thought: Indeed, the matter is known. Pharaoh heard
about this matter and sought to kill Moses; so Moses

fled from before Pharaoh and settled in the land of Midian. And he sat by the well. The minister of Midian had seven daughters; they came and drew water and filled the troughs to water their father's sheep. The shepherds came and drove them away. Moses got up and saved them and watered their sheep. They came to Reuel, their father, and he said: How could you come so quickly today? They replied: An Egyptian *man* saved us from the shepherds and he even drew water for us and watered the sheep. He said to his daughters: Then where is he? Why did you leave the *man?* Summon him and let him eat bread. And Moses desired to dwell with the *man,* and he gave his daughter Zipporah to Moses. She gave birth to a son and he named him Gershom, for he said: I have been a stranger in a foreign land. (Exodus 2:11–22)

Here the word "man" is repeated seven times (six in the last half of the section and once in the first sentence of the section). Notice that while the latter half of this section deals with the man Moses, only twice does the word "man" refer to him, the other five times "man" refers to other men. The code nevertheless is preserved. As the child–man development of Moses is narrated, the Seven Code insinuates the text with the same message.

Tuning In to the Code Word

We must listen to the cadence and rhythm of the text. When we learn to do this, the wordplays stand out boldly. It is no coincidence that the first scholar to write about the Seven Code was blind. He wrote that his inability to follow the Torah reading by sight made him more sensitive to its sounds.

Noticing the word density is very important. This means that when words repeat themselves in close proximity, this is an indication that the Seven Code may be at hand.

The following illustrates this point.

Example 6—Cain and Abel, Brothers

And Adam knew Eve his wife; and she became pregnant and bare Cain, and said, I have obtained a man from the Lord. And she again bare his *brother* Abel. And Abel was a shepherd of flocks, but Cain was a tiller of the soil. And in process of time it came to pass that Cain brought of the fruit of the ground an oblation to the Lord. And Abel also brought of the firstborn of his flock and of the fat thereof. And the Lord had regard to Abel and his oblation. But to Cain and to his oblation He had not regard. And Cain was very wroth, and his face fell. And the Lord said to Cain, Why are you wroth? and why is your face fallen? Is it not thus, if you mend, there is forgiveness and if you do not mend, sin crouches at the entrance. And to you is its longing, nevertheless you may rule over it. And Cain said to Abel his *brother:* and it came to pass, when they were in the field, that Cain rose up against Abel his *brother,* and killed him. And the Lord said to Cain, Where is Abel your *brother?* And he said, I know not. Am I my *brother*'s keeper? And He said, What have you done? the voice of your *brother*'s blood cries unto me from the ground. And now cursed are you from the ground, which has opened her mouth to take your *brother*'s blood from your hand. (Genesis 4:1–11)

The code word "brother" is repeated in close proximity six times in four sentences. This is an example of word density.

At times the Seven Code is much harder to detect, but uncovering it can explain textual peculiarities, which otherwise would remain a conundrum.

Example 7—From Adam to Noah

The German scholar Goldberg has enlightened us about one such puzzle. In Genesis, chapter 5, where the ten generations between Adam and Noah are enumerated, the final sentence of each section (which gives a brief account of each man's life) ends with "And all the days of . . . were. . . ." In Hebrew, the word is *VaYiheyu,* meaning "and they (days) were." Yet, in two instances, the singular *VaYehi* ("and it was") is used. The table will make it clear.

Adam	(5:5)	*Vayiheyu*	
Sheth	(5:8)	"	
Enosh	(5:11)	"	
Kenan	(5:14)	"	
Mehalalel	(5:17)	"	
Yered	(5:20)	"	
Hanoch	(5:23)		*Vayehi*
Methushela	(5:27)	"	
Lemech	(5:31)		*Vayehi*
Noah	(9:29)		*Vayehi*
		7	3

While Noah's name is not mentioned until several chapters later, the continuity of the code is preserved—the Seven Code as well as the Ten Code, which we saw in the chapter in Exodus about the Tablets.

This is certainly a strange textual phenomenon. Nevertheless, it does show us that there is method behind what appears to be compositional capriciousness. Consequently once we see the Seven Code pattern at work, we can interpret textual idiosyncrasies in a rational way.

11

An Exercise in In-Depth Interpretation: The Ten Plagues

In the following chapters I will apply techniques of In-Depth Interpretation to two full-length accounts in the Torah. My intent is to show how probing a variety of textual nuances allows us entrance into the multi-layered levels of meaning submerged within the Scriptural record. Plain Sense interpretation will have the cumulative effect of revealing a breathtaking panorama of Torah insights.

The two longest sagas in the Torah are those of Joseph and his brothers, in Genesis, and of the Exodus from Egypt—including the Ten Plagues and Pharaoh's obstinate refusal to set the Jews free, as recorded in the Book of Exodus. It is not by chance that these two dramas take center stage in the Pentateuch; they epitomize the two main currents which run throughout the whole of Jewish history—Exile and Redemption.

We take as our first text the familiar story of the Ten Plagues which God visited upon Pharaoh and his people as the prelude to the Jews' Exodus from Egypt.

133

I pointed out earlier that the *What* and *How* of the text
are our bases for interpretation. In the discussion that
follows, the burden of interpretation falls nearly exclusively on *What* the text says. This is unusual, because it
implies that the deeper meanings are right in front of our
eyes. We need only see what we read to become aware of
them. That we often don't see what we read, I think, will
become apparent from the analysis that follows. Again we
are committed to the text alone, bound by it and emanci-
pated by it at the same time.

In reviewing this story we will discuss its three different levels:

1. The story as usually understood
2. The deeper meaning of the story
3. The deeper significance of this meaning

Let us start with a problematic text, Exodus 9:13:

And the Eternal said to Moses, "Rise up early in the
morning, and place yourself before Pharaoh, and say
to him, Thus saith the Eternal God of the Hebrews,
Let My people go, that they may serve Me. For I
will at this time send all My plagues upon your heart,
and upon your servants, and upon your people; that
you may know that there is none like Me in all the
earth. For now I might have stretched out My hand,
and I might have smitten you and your people with
pestilence; and you would have been exterminated
from the earth. But indeed for this purpose have I
raised you up in order to show you My power and so
that My name will be declared throughout the earth.
You still trample My people, not letting them go.

Behold, tomorrow at this time I will cause a rain of very heavy hail, such as has not been seen in Egypt from the day of its foundation even until now. Send therefore now, and gather your cattle, and all you have in the fields; for every man and every beast which shall be found in the field and shall not be gathered into the house, the hail shall come down upon them and they shall die.'' He that feared the word of the Eternal among the servants of Pharaoh made his servants and his cattle flee into the houses. And he that did not regard the word of the Eternal left his servants and his cattle in the field.

A close examination of this text raises several questions. I will take them one by one.

1. ''This time I will send *all My plagues* on your heart'' (verse 14). In what way are we to understand that the plague of hail is equivalent to *all My plagues?* Commentators have struggled with this question.

2. ''For this reason have I let you stand, to show you My power and that My *name shall be declared* throughout the Earth.'' This is the only one of the Ten Plagues where declaring God's Name is mentioned. Does this phrase have any significance? What might it be?

3. Why does this plague merit such a long introduction—the longest of all the plagues? Longer even than the introduction to the final and decisive plague of the killing of the firstborn.

4. Pharaoh uncharacteristically confesses, ''I have sinned this time.'' This is the first time he admits to having sinned. Why does he do so at this juncture?

A casual reading of this section would pass off these questions as pedantic sophistry. Most of us are not accustomed to reading the Scriptures with such demands of accountable coherency. Yet it is precisely by making such demands and knowing how to search for answers that a familiar text transforms before our eyes into a fascinating adventure.

To answer our questions, we must take a broader view of the whole story of the plagues.

The Purpose of the Plagues

How are we to understand the purpose of the plagues? On the surface, it would seem that they are God's method of subduing Pharaoh and forcing him into letting the Jews go free. But were this their main purpose, why the necessity for all of them? God could have brought Pharaoh to his knees immediately with the killing of the firstborn, as He did eventually. In fact, God told Moses (Exodus 4:22–23) at the very outset of the struggle:

> And you should say to Pharaoh, Thus says the Eternal, Israel is My son, My firstborn. And I say to you, Let My son go, that he may serve Me; and if you refuse to let him go, behold, I will slay your son, your firstborn.

In spite of the prior knowledge that only the killing of Pharaoh's firstborn would bring about redemption, God nevertheless leads Pharaoh through the labyrinth of the Ten Plagues. Accordingly, we can't view the contest between God and Pharaoh as merely a display of Divine power pitted against human strength.

Our clue to the deeper meaning comes from a close reading of the text. At the very first meeting between Moses and Pharaoh (Exodus 5:1–2), we read:

> And afterwards Moses and Aaron came, and said to Pharaoh, Thus says the Eternal, (the Ineffable Name) the God of Israel, Let My People go, that they may celebrate for Me in the desert. And Pharaoh said, *Who is the Eternal* that I should obey His voice to let Israel go? *I know not the Eternal* and neither will I let Israel go.

In this first encounter, two opposing stands are clearly defined. Moses asks for the Jews' freedom in the name of the Eternal, so that they may serve Him. And Pharaoh defiantly rebuffs the petition by undermining the basis of Moses' authority: "Who is the Eternal . . . I know not the Eternal! [hence] I will not let Israel go."

Pharaoh's thundering, "I know not the Eternal," serves as the foil against which the series of plagues are played out. Their ultimate, albeit implicit, purpose then is to teach Pharaoh who the Eternal is. That this, in fact, is the goal of the plagues, more so even than the actual freeing of the Jews, can be seen from Exodus 7:4. When Moses prepares to go to Pharaoh after his first rejection we are told:

> But Pharaoh will not listen to you and I will lay My hand on Egypt and bring forth My hosts, My children of Israel, out of the land of Egypt by great judgments. And *Egypt will know that I am the eternal. . . .*

We see clearly that letting the Jews go free was only the penultimate goal, while educating Pharaoh and his people

as to who The Eternal is, was the ultimate purpose of the
plagues. Grasping the cosmological significance of the
reality that the Eternal is the master of history was not a
means to having Pharaoh succumb to His omnipotent will
and free the Jews; rather Pharaoh's coerced letting-go was
to be an object lesson in comprehending who the Eternal
is. Notice that the words, "You will know, (They will
know) that I am the Eternal," are repeated no less than ten
times throughout this drama.

The Lesson Plan

A closer review of the whole story of the plagues reveals a
magnificent lesson plan for teaching this message. The
plagues and their warnings begin in Exodus 7:17, with the
plague of blood and end with Moses' last encounter with
Pharaoh before the final plague of the killing of the firstborn in Exodus 11:4. An examination of the plagues and
their warnings discloses an intricately designed matrix
with the following features:

The plagues are divided into three groups of three each
(1,2,3 . . . 4,5,6 . . . 7,8,9, and 10), with the final plague,
killing of the firstborn, standing by itself. The three divisions have identical structures.

Plagues 1, 4, and 7, being the first of each grouping, all
begin with meeting Pharaoh in the morning (Exodus 7:15,
8:16, and 9:13), usually as he goes to the river.

Plagues 2, 5, and 8, the second of each grouping (Exodus 7:27, 9:1, and 10:1), all begin with the phrase
"Come to Pharaoh . . . ," implying a palace visit.

Plagues 3, 6, and 9, the last of each group, have no
warnings to Pharaoh at all. These plagues (lice, boils,

and darkness) come on suddenly with no prior warning by Moses.

This alone is remarkable. But of more significance is that each grouping of three has its own special introduction, with the shared theme of knowing the Eternal.

Plague 1—"Thus says the Eternal, With this you will *know* that *I am the Eternal*" (Exodus 7:17).

Plague 4—" . . . In order that you will *know* that *I am the Eternal in the midst of the earth*" (Exodus 8:22).

Plague 7—" . . . In order that you will *know* that *there is none like unto Me in all the earth*" (Exodus 9:14).

The commentaries (Abarbanel, Malbim) have pointed out the three levels of knowledge of the Eternal:

First, that He exists.
Second, that He involves Himself in earthly matters.
And third, that He is unequaled in His sovereignty in this world.

Thus we see how a theological theme and variation are artfully woven into the story of the plagues. The theme, as we have shown, is that the Eternal exists, that He is involved in worldly matters, and that the nature of His involvement in this world is unique. This, then, is the meaning of the story. It might fittingly be dubbed "A Crash Course in Jewish Theology."

But what, we may ask, is the significance of all this? What can Pharaoh know about the Eternal, other than that He is omnipotent and that He has His own unique, ineffable, name? What do we moderns know, for that

matter, about the significance of the Jewish God's uniqueness? To the outside observer, He is but another divin-
ity in the overcrowded pantheon of divinities of the
ancient world.

It was while introducing the plague of hail that Moses
said, " . . . in order that you declare *My Name* throughout the earth." Why? And why this plague?

Answering these questions will lead us to uncovering
the magnificent message of this apparently simple story, a
message which is a groundbreaking theological contribution of monotheistic Judaism.

Let us look again at the seventh plague, where our
questions began. I pointed out several difficulties, the
most puzzling being: Why is this plague referred to as "all
My plagues"? One possible answer can now be given.
Since this is the first of the last of three groupings of
plagues, perhaps the Torah means: The final group of
plagues with which the pummeling of Pharaoh and his
people will finally come to an end.

The Significance of the Plagues

But the Torah suggests a deeper explanation. Let us take
the last question we asked: Why did Pharaoh admit now,
for the first time, that "I have sinned this time. The
Eternal is the righteous one; and I and my people are the
evil ones"? To answer this question we must note what is
unique about the plague of hail. Every plague was presented to Pharaoh as an ultimatum: He could either com-
ply and let the Jews free or suffer the plague—*except* for
the plague of hail. Here it says:

Send, therefore, now and gather the cattle and all you have in the field. For every man and animal which shall be found in the field and not gathered into the house, the hail shall come upon them and they will die.

Here, for the first and only time, God offers Pharaoh a choice which does not require of him total capitulation. To escape the punishment and plague, all that is necessary is for the people to stay inside during the hailstorm. Considering God's unlimited options, this is certainly a reasonable and fair bargain. And so it says:

He that feared the word of the Eternal among the servants of Pharaoh made his servants and cattle flee into the houses. But he who paid no attention to the word of the Eternal left his servants and cattle in the field. (Exodus 9:19–20)

It is for this reason that at this point, and not until now, that Pharaoh recognized the Eternal's mercy and right-eousness. With this equitable choice, God showed Pha-raoh His merciful side and not His punitive side.

Granting the fact that the Eternal acted mercifully when warning of the plague of hail, is this sufficient reason to consider it ''all My Plagues'' and to warrant the longest introduction of any of the plagues? We think not. The explanation is to be found in a most subtle nuance in the text of this story. We quote from Exodus 9:27:

And Pharaoh sent, and called for Moses and Aaron, and said to them, I have sinned this time; the Eternal is righteous, and I and my people are wicked. Entreat

to the Eternal for there have been too many thunder-
ings of God and hail; and I will let you go and you
will stay no longer. And Moses said to him: As soon as
I have gone out of the city, I will spread my hands to
the Eternal; the thunder will cease, neither will there
be any more hail; that you may know that the earth
belongs to the Eternal. But as for you and your servants, I know that you will not yet be afraid of The
Eternal, God.

The last words, "The Eternal, God" (The Tetragrammaton, God), as used here, are remarkably unique. Certainly the Tetragrammaton is used innumerable times
throughout the Bible and it is frequently joined by such
adjectives as "Our God," "Your God." But this particular
phrase is a singular anomaly. Nowhere else in the Torah do
we find a person using the Tetragrammaton coupled with
the noun "God."

When we say "the Eternal (the ineffable Name), our
God," the words "our God" are an adjective, describing
the noun, Eternal. On the other hand, were we to say
"Eternal, God," then the latter term is another noun,
parallel to Eternal and not an adjective describing the
term Eternal.

To clarify the significance of this point, some explanation is necessary. We know that the various names of God
in the Torah have different meanings (see the beginning of
Exodus, chapter 6). "The Eternal" (the Tetragrammaton)
reflects Divine Mercy while "God" (Elohim) signifies
Divine Judgment, the stern hand of Justice. The latter
Hebrew term is also used in the Bible for "judge."

The Ibn Ezra points out elsewhere in his commentary
(Exodus 3:13) that nowhere in the Torah are the names

the Eternal (the ineffable Name) and Elohim spoken together by Moses. Nowhere in the whole Torah—*except* here! This is much too striking an exception to be a mere coincidence.

This fact is all the more remarkable when we consider how often people utter the names of God throughout the Torah. For example, in the Book of Deuteronomy, where Moses gives his final oration to the people, he repeatedly mentions the Divine names, such as "the Eternal our God," "the Eternal your God." Never once does he use the phrase "the Eternal, God."

The meaning of this nearly imperceptible message seems to be that the two Divine names cannot be brought together because they represent two diametrically opposed and mutually incompatible characteristics. Mercy is the abrogation of Justice; Justice is the implementation of law, regardless of whether it is merciful or not. The two terms are like two positive magnets which repel each other. Thus man cannot utter these two Divine appellations, because he cannot conceive of them together as compatible traits. We only find them juxtaposed in the Torah when God himself is speaking, as in the Creation story, for example.

In summary, then, the term "Eternal/God" translates to mean "The Merciful/Just One"—an oxymoron. One which the human mind cannot grasp.

Only once in the whole Pentateuch is that "taboo" broken and man utters this ineffable contradiction—here at the seventh plague of hail! In a masterly orchestrated symphony of subtlety, the Torah uses the plague of hail to symbolize the Mercy/Justice contradiction, both in a concrete and a poetic way. In a concrete way, we saw that only with this plague did God offer Pharaoh a merciful "way out," a fair option to avoid the lethal plague without being forced to free the Jews upon whom his economy depended. Only those Egyptians who stubbornly "paid no attention to the word of the Eternal" were justly punished.

And notice how the plague of hail hammers home the same message in poetic fashion. The plague was actually hail mixed with fire: "So there was hail and consuming fire in the midst of the hail . . . " (Exodus 9:24). Hail and fire are a double contradiction, or, if you will, an enigma wrapped in a mystery (see Rashi on this sentence). Fire melts the ice of hail, thus transforming it into water. And water, in turn, extinguishes fire. The two can't abide together for long; they will either transform or destroy each other—like Mercy and Justice! To the human mind, they can't abide together; only Divine power can accomplish such a feat. This is a dazzling metaphor of poetic justice. Here we have scriptural symbolism at its best.

The theme of balancing Mercy and Justice is interwoven throughout this story. It can also be seen from the fact that of the ten places where "knowing the Eternal" is mentioned, five of these instances concern acts of God that were intended to save the Jews or stop a plague (i.e., offering mercy), while the other five occur when He comes to punish the Egyptians (implementing justice). Again, an even balance between Mercy and Justice.

We now see the significance of the phrase "So you will tell My Name throughout the land." God's names here reflect His unique character, His ability to balance Mercy and Justice in His dealings with this world. This, then, is the significance, the meaning behind the meaning, the ultimate object-lesson of the plagues and, most graphically, of the plague of hail.

It is for this reason that this plague is considered "all My plagues." It alone embodies manifestly and symbolically the message of all the plagues. Thus, it merited the longest introduction of all the plagues. And, of course, didn't you notice? This is the seventh plague, no less! (see chapter 10, The Seven Code).

We see with this example how various levels of interlocking meaning are blended into the text. But most important to note, for our purposes, is that all these complementary and supplementary levels of meaning are revealed to us within the manifest text itself, the Plain Sense, *P'shat,* level of understanding. These deeper meanings of *P'shat* become available to us by careful reading and attentive listening to the text itself. The Plain Sense interpretation strives to detect each and every nuance in the text and to explain its purpose within the larger context of the Torah's message.

The questions formulated at the outset of this chapter flow naturally from an attitude of critical reverence for the comprehensibility of the text. The interpretive work consisted of making use of the many textual hints (originally posed as questions), seeing them in their larger context, and searching for a comprehensive explanation. In this way we enable the story to open up its hidden treasures to us.

We take away from this in-depth exercise in interpretation one primary lesson: The more we become sensitive to difficulties in the text, no matter how minor they may first seem to be, the more opportunity we have for uncovering their deeper meaning.

12

The Joseph Story: Textual Discontinuity, Thematic Continuity

A view of the Scriptures as a unified whole enables us to better understand its individual parts. Though the Hebrew Scriptures are composed of twenty-four books which span a history of over 3,000 years, woven throughout it are grand themes which connect diverse parts and create a unified whole. There are interconnecting threads, camouflaged but not imperceptible, which stretch across generations and across chapters and books of the Scriptures. When discerned, they reveal a breathtaking tapestry of meaning. Our purpose, in this book, is to show the various aspects of Plain Sense interpretation and how an in-depth analysis affords us not only an appreciation of the text per se, but a deeper understanding of the biblical view of man and history. For our second full-length illustration of this, we have chosen the story of Joseph and his brothers. As a starting point we will focus on a puzzling non sequitur within that story.

The story of Joseph and his brothers is the longest recorded theme in the Torah, covering some twenty-two chapters. That is evidence enough of its importance. It is a story that stands on its own as a supreme literary achievement; the struggles between the sons of Jacob are portrayed with psychological sophistication, dramatic dialogue, and plot development that builds to a crescendo of pent-up emotions. But the story's literary artistry exists not only for its own sake. Its purpose as part of the Scriptures is to enable us to see behind the manifest human drama the guiding hand of Divine intention. Although never mentioned in the text itself, the influence of Divine Providence resounds loud and clear.

Before we start our examination of the story, it is advisable for the reader to review the relevant chapters (especially Genesis, chapters 37–45) several times. The more familiar we are with the material the more sensitive we become to its finer points.

The Story-Theme

In broadest terms (leaving out several sub-plots), the story of Joseph and his brothers can be summarized as follows:

In an intricate causal chain of events, the children of Jacob are taken from what could have been a tranquil life in the land of Canaan to the beginning of exile in the land of Egypt. The steps leading to this downfall are clearly recorded in the Torah (Genesis, chapters 37–45), beginning with Jacob's preference for Rachel's firstborn son, Joseph; this, plus Joseph's dreams of family leadership, lead to the brothers' jealousy and their plan to kill him. Instead, Joseph is sold into slavery in Egypt where, by means of his ability to interpret dreams, he rises to the position of Viceroy of Egypt. The years of famine which

Joseph predicted give him power over the Egyptians and the surrounding countries. The famine hits Canaan also and Jacob's sons go down to Egypt to buy food from Joseph, whom they don't recognize. After Joseph reveals his true identity to his dumbfounded brothers, he arranges for his father and brothers to settle in Egypt. This is the first generation of Jews to live in Exile; it marks the beginning of what is to become a severe Exile. This Exile of destructive discrimination, wanton aggression, sexual exploitation, and eventually genocide was to prove to be the paradigm for future Exiles that the Jews were to live through.

The Problem

The story is clear enough, its drama moving, and its denouement spellbinding. All parts of the story fit together and make sense in light of its eventual conclusion. All, that is, except for Genesis, chapter 38, the story of Judah and Tamar. This is the story of Judah, his marriage to the businessman Shua's daughter, the birth of three sons, the marriage of the two older sons to Tamar, their death, then Judah's relationship with Tamar, and the birth of the twins Peretz and Zerach from this union. The interjection of this chapter into the middle of the story of the sale of Joseph, with no explanation, is a puzzling non sequitur.

Re-reading the last sentence in Genesis, chapter 37, and the first one of chapter 39, we see how inappropriate the inserted chapter is: "And the Medanim sold him to Egypt to Potiphar, a captain of Pharaoh's, officer of the executioners." This ends chapter 37. Then comes the story of Judah and Tamar. Then chapter 39 begins picking up directly from chapter 37: "And Joseph was brought down to Egypt; and Potiphar, a captain of Pharaoh, officer of the executioners, an Egyptian man, obtained him from the hands of the Ishmaelites, who had brought him down thither."

It looks like a mechanical insertion, an inappropriate and artificial addition—a gross redactor's error, if you will—a significant oral tradition that had to be shoehorned in somewhere. But appreciation for the Torah's craft in composition, attention to meaningful detail, and talent for embedded messages behooves us to understand the meaning of this strange phenomenon.

The Second Theme

To enable us to get a fuller perspective of the Torah's message, we need to point out a second theme that parallels the descent into Exile theme, that is, the rivalry for leadership among the sons of Jacob. The struggle between Joseph and his brothers is not just a case of sibling rivalry; it is no less than the struggle for the mantle of leadership for the future of nation Israel. Jacob's sons were fully aware that of Abraham's two sons, only one had been chosen—Isaac. Of Isaac's two sons, only one had been chosen—Jacob. Of Jacob's sons, they certainly wondered, who would be chosen and who excluded? This tension is the backdrop to the strong emotions that cloud the relations between the brothers.

A careful reading of all the chapters dealing with Joseph and the brothers (Genesis, chapters 37–49) will show a noteworthy fact: The Torah quotes only three of the twelve sons by name; the three are Reuben, Judah, and

Joseph. They are locked in a historic struggle for the leadership, kingship, of the People of Israel. Reuben is Jacob's firstborn and thus the rightful heir; Joseph is Rachel's firstborn and, for this reason, Jacob's favorite; Judah has no inherited rights to leadership yet his strength of character may be the most fitting for such an awesome responsibility. These three are engaged in an ongoing contest which the Torah allows us to witness. We see the differences in their personalities etched into the interactions between them. From these differences we get an understanding of how a leader is chosen and what spiritual characteristics qualify him to lead the People of Israel.

When the brothers see Joseph coming to meet them, Reuben is the first brother to be quoted: "And Reuben said to them, Don't spill blood. Throw him into the pit which is in the wilderness and let not a hand be sent against him; in order to save him from their hands, to return him to his father" (Genesis 37:22). There is no response from his brothers. This may imply that, while his suggestion was heeded, they didn't give Reuben much credit for it.

After the brothers remove themselves from the pit and sit down to eat, Judah addresses them; "And Judah said to his brothers: What gain is there if we kill our brother and cover his blood? Let us sell him to the Ishmaelites, and our hands will not be against him, for he is our brother, our flesh. *And the brothers accepted.*"

We see here that it is Judah's advice that is taken over that of Reuben's. The text says, "The brothers accepted (listen to)" Judah; not so when Reuben speaks.

Later on (Genesis 42:37) when Jacob refuses to send his youngest son, Benjamin, with the brothers to buy food, Reuben tries to convince him: "And Reuben said to his father: My two sons you may kill if I don't bring him [Benjamin] back to you." Jacob is unmoved. Later Judah intercedes: "And Judah said to Israel his father, Send the lad with me and we will go and we will live and not die . . . I guarantee him, from my hand can you claim him, if I don't bring him to you and place him before you, I will have sinned to you all the days." After these words of Judah, Jacob immediately concedes to sending Benjamin. Again we see that Judah's word is more influential than Reuben's.

And it is Judah, not Reuben, who steps forth to intercede with Joseph. It is his poignant plea for Benjamin (Genesis 44:18–34) that finally causes Joseph to reveal himself to his brothers. Compare this with Reuben's remark to his brothers (Genesis 42:22), which causes Joseph to cry but does not move him enough to reveal himself, as he later did when Judah spoke up. Again Judah's assertiveness is skilled enough to accomplish his goal. In so doing, he exemplifies the qualities of leadership.

To summarize these two motifs, we have the theme of the fledgling People of Israel going down to Egypt-Exile and we have the theme of the struggle among the brothers for leadership of the People of Israel.

A Closer Look at the Puzzling Chapter 38

Genesis, chapter 38, begins with the words "And it was at that time that Judah went down from his brothers. . . ." We can assume it was at the time that Joseph was sold. Yet the events portrayed in this chapter—Judah leaving his brothers and marrying a foreign woman, having three sons, marrying the first two off to Tamar, their premature deaths, Judah's widowhood, him having relations with an unknown woman (who is Tamar in disguise), then Tamar's pregnancy, and the birth of twins—all of this must have taken place in the course of several years. Even if we assume that the story began at the time of Joseph's sale, it certainly didn't all transpire between Joseph being sold and him arriving in Egypt. Yet that is where it is placed in the Torah, right between "And the Medanim sold Joseph to the Egyptians" and the first sentence of chapter 39, "And Joseph was brought down to Egypt . . ." Some reason other than a chronological one must be the basis for the insertion at this point in the longer Joseph story.

The Torah gives us several clues, imbedded within the story which enable us to find links between the chapters. Here the *Midrash Rabbah* leads us to these clues:

> "And Judah sent the kid of the goats to take the deposit from the woman's hand, but found her not." Judah, son of Nachman, said in the name of Reish Lakish, "She (the Torah) plays with the habitants of his world, plays before him at all times (Proverbs 8:31)." The Torah plays with the creatures. The Holy One said to Judah: You deceived your father with a goat, (putting Joseph's colored coat in the goat's blood to show to Jacob). By your life! Tamar will deceive you with a goat.

The Hebrew word *Eizim,* "goat," is repeated both in this section and the previous one about Joseph and his brothers. The word *eizim,* used in the case of Joseph's kidnapping and again in the story of Judah and Tamar, forms a clear word association drawing our attention to the connection between these two events.

The Midrash continues to stitch the two chapters together:

"And she (Tamar) said: Recognize (*Haker Na*) whose are these, the signet . . ." (Genesis 38:25). Said Rav Yochanan, "Said the Holy One Blessed be He to Judah: You said to your father (Genesis 37:32), Recognize (*Haker Na*) is this your son's tunic or not?" By your life! Tamar will also say to you, *Haker Na* (Recognize)!

This play on words is by no means trivial; the words *Haker Na* appear in the whole Scriptures only twice, here in Tamar's speech to Judah and in the previous chapter in Judah's speech to his father, Jacob. We see a clear verbal association between the two chapters. What sense can we make out of this association? The moral lesson seems to be: Deception is paid back in the same coin—deception. Judah had deceived his father with his disingenuous *Haker Na;* now Tamar confronts Judah and uncovers her deception of him (as a harlot) with the trauma-laden words *Haker Na.*

The Midrash goes further and enlightens us to a more profound truth. We can relish the poetry of the Midrash.

"And it was at that time," Rav Shmuel, son of Nachman, opened his talk: "Because I know the thoughts which I think about them . . . to give them hope and a successful end" (Jeremiah 29:11). The tribes were busy selling Joseph; Joseph was busy with his sackcloth and fasting [because he was sold into slavery]; Reuben was occupied with his sackcloth and fasting

[referring to the incident with Jacob's concubine Bil-
hah (Genesis 35:22)]; Jacob was occupied with his
sackcloth and fasting [due to the loss of Joseph];
Judah was busy taking a wife, and The Holy One was
occupied with . . . creating the light of the Messiah.
"And it was at that time. . . ."

What is the meaning of this strange Midrash? Everyone
was busy doing his own thing and the Holy One was busy
creating the light of the Messiah! As if to say that the Holy
One was desperately searching for someone to be His
agent to implement His will in history, but all were preoc-
cupied with their own problems. Nevertheless, He found
a way to accomplish His goal. That goal: Creating the
Messiah. What is this Midrash telling us about the story of
Judah and Tamar?

The meaning becomes clear when we look at the conclusion of the Judah/Tamar story. At the end of Genesis,
chapter 38, we read that Tamar, who was waiting to fulfill
the levirate rite and marry her brother-in-law, became
pregnant. For having relations with someone other than
her brother-in-law, Judah, her father-in-law, sentences her
to death. She is brought out and discloses, privately, to
Judah that she is pregnant by him.

And Judah recognized (*VaYaker*) and he said: She is
more righteous than I; it is because I haven't given
her to Shelah my son. And he did not continue to
know her. And it was at the time of her birth and she
had twins. And it was when she gave birth and he put
out a hand. And the midwife took it and tied on his
hand a crimson thread, saying: This one came out
first. And when he withdrew his hand and, behold,

his brother went out. And she said: How did you burst
forth? This bursting upon you! And he called his name
Peretz. Afterwards his brother came out, on his hand
the crimson thread. And he called his name Zerach.
(Genesis 38:26–30)

Thus the story ends. The episode of Judah and Tamar is
complete. Very unusual! For the Torah never relates matters that have no significance. What then, is the significance of the birth of Zerach and Peretz? They never
appear again in the Torah except in brief genealogical
tables. Does the whole, strange (sordid?) story of Judah's
"going down" culminate in the birth of these two boys?
We are left hanging.

The Interpretation (Solution)

Our answer is to be found within the scriptural text itself,
but this time not within the Five Books of Moses; it is in
the Book of Ruth, which relates events that occurred
centuries later.

The story of Ruth the Moabite took place in the period of
the Judges, hundreds of years after the events of Joseph and
his brothers, which are portrayed in Genesis. The short
book of Ruth culminates in the marriage of Ruth to Boaz
and the birth of their son: "And they called him Oved. He
is the father of Yeshai, the father of David" (Ruth 4:17).

These are the generations of Peretz:

Peretz begat Hezron;
Hezron begat Ram;
Ram begat Amminadab; and

Amminadab begat Nahshon; and
Nahshon begat Salmah; and
Salmon begat Boaz; and
Boaz begat Obed. And
Obed begat Jesse; and
Jesse begat David
                    (Ruth 4:18–22)

The story of Ruth is climaxed by the announcement that David, King of Israel, the Messiah, was her offspring. David's predecessors are mentioned through Boaz all the way back to Peretz. But why stop there? Why not back to Judah? This would be the logical conclusion, since David was of the tribe of Judah.

It suggests that the reason the Book of Ruth highlights Peretz is the same reason that the Book of Genesis ends the Judah/Tamar affair with Peretz's birth. The point is to lead us to free-associate—Peretz . . . Peretz. When we read of David's genealogy and hear Peretz's name, we think back to the last significant time Peretz was mentioned, at the conclusion of the Judah/Tamar story. And when we read of Peretz in the Judah/Tamar story we think forward to the Book of Ruth. Peretz's name becomes associated with the birth of David, the Messiah! Thus our midrashic message of God creating the light of the Messiah is clarified.

Conclusion

The significance of the story of Judah's "going down" and its relevance to the sale of Joseph into exile is now clear. His actions were the raw material for the creation of the Messiah (Peretz . . . Boaz . . . David). The story in

Genesis ends with the birth of Peretz because this is all we
need to know in order to understand the word association, "Peretz . . . Peretz," and thus see its place in the
foretelling of the birth of the Redeemer of Israel.

This is what the Rabbis meant when they said, "The
Holy One was occupied with creating the light of the
Messiah." The beauty and profundity of this Midrash is
thrilling. See how Genesis, chapter 38, was placed precisely after the sale of Joseph yet *before* he actually enters
Egypt. Egypt signifies the Jewish Exile, Judah's "going
down" signifies the birth of David, the Jewish Redeemer.
As the Rabbis were wont to say, "The Holy One creates the
medicine before the illness." The message being: Though
the People of Israel are entering Exile, their Redeemer is
already born. Eventual Redemption is Divinely guaran-
teed. By means of an artfully constructed literary device,
the apparent non sequitur of Genesis, chapter 38, the
Torah finds a subtle vehicle for conveying a fundamental
tenet of Jewish belief.

Summary

The above interpretation of Genesis, chapter 38, is offered as an example of *P'shat*-analysis and interpretation,
even though it is based to a great extent on the *Midrashim*
of the rabbinic Sages. The use of Midrash for Plain Sense
interpretation is perfectly acceptable for, while the Midrash is generally comprised of Drash (a different mode
of interpretation from *P'shat*), it may also contain the
other modes of Torah interpretation—*Remez, Sode,* and
P'shat. The reason I consider this within the realm of
P'shat interpretation should be clear by now. The en-

tire interpretation, the various elements that were analyzed, and the suggested solution *all came from the text alone, the text in its context.* This example illustrates how the story-theme contains within it the Torah's theology of history, Exile and Redemption, man's actions, and Divine involvement.

The search for, and attention to, the nuances of the text, the verbal associations imbedded within it, and the vital significance of every detail all enable us to reap the ultimate benefit of a comprehensive *P'shat* analysis—uncovering the Scriptures' deeper messages.

13

The Messianic Personality— Reverberations through the Scriptures

In the previous chapter, I have shown that the apparently self-contained chapter on Judah and Tamar is not self-contained at all. It projects its word-associations across chapters and across generations, alerting us to the deeper meanings of the text, meanings that would have eluded us had we not kept an open mind and ear to connections within the Scriptures as a whole.

The 38th chapter of Genesis sends out other fascinating reverberations through the Bible in a way that reveals a biblical view of the Messianic personality. Gossamer threads are stretched across the Scriptures, so delicate that only dedicated study prevents their evading detection. Picking up these threads, unraveling their direction, and deciphering their message is a thrilling experience. Personally, I have found no equal to it for intellectual gratification and spiritual exhilaration.

What I am about to discuss in this short chapter is the discovery of an example of a consistency throughout the

Scriptures, which is based not on some literary device but rather on a psychological-historical-moral reality that translates itself into a powerful biblical message. This the Bible does in its own inimitable way.

Viewing the Bible as literature has its benefits, but it can also subject us to tunnel vision. The benefits, which the classical Torah commentators made maximum use of without necessarily viewing them merely as "literary" devices (like the man who spoke prose all his life without realizing it), have been amply illustrated in earlier chapters of this book. We must state, however, that the commentators realized that the Scriptures teach their messages in ways other than by literary devices. They also teach by example of the personalities depicted in them.

Among the many virtuosities of the Torah's literary style is its ability to portray individual personality traits with a minimum of detail. As I illustrated in the chapter on the Psychological Dimension, we see a consistency of character across different episodes in the lives of both Moses and Saul. The Torah's ability to bring personalities to life with the barest of sketches is remarkable, to say the least. In the story of Judah and Tamar we are witness to an even more remarkable phenomenon. We see how a particular character trait is transmitted from generation to generation. I am referring to what the Torah appears to take as the essential personality trait of the Messiah, the leader of Israel. I have pointed out how the Judah-Tamar text had as its covert message the birth of the Messiah. Because of the Judah-Tamar affair, Judah became the forebearer of David, King of Israel.

Besides Judah's obvious leadership qualities, which come to the fore in his confrontation with Joseph (Genesis 44:18–34), another aspect of Judah's personality is revealed in his relationship with Tamar.

> And it came to pass about three months after, that it was told to Judah, saying, Tamar thy daughter-in-law hath played the harlot, and also, behold, she is pregnant by fornication. And Judah said, Bring her forth and let her burn. When she was brought forth, she sent to her husband's father saying, By the man whose these are am I pregnant: and she said, Recognize, I pray thee whose are these, the signet and strings and staff. And Judah recognized them and said, She hath been more righteous than I; because I gave her not to Shelah my son. And he knew her no more. (Genesis 38:24–26)

What catches our eye here is Judah's unhesitating admission of guilt. Let's remember it was her word against his. He was in the position of power from any point of view—Man versus Woman; Elder versus Youth; and Father versus Daughter. He could have also rationalized that if Tamar slept with him who knows how many other men she may have slept with. Thus, Judah could have easily condemned her to death for other assumed infidelities.

In spite of the cards being decidedly stacked in his favor, we find Judah making an admission of guilt which is unqualified, uncompromising, and unexcusing of himself. Instead he finds justification for Tamar's act of "infidelity" and blames himself for it: "because I gave her not to Shelah my son."

In light of all we know today about the corruption of power and how common it is, even in democratic governments, for those in power, be they attorney generals,

presidents, or prime ministers, to deny guilt for any but
the most innocuous peccadilloes, Judah's act stands out
boldly. This ability, for a leader who need answer to no
one, to honestly admit his guilt and forthrightly take
responsibility for his actions is *the* moral fiber that must
characterize the King of Israel.

Denial of guilt, the shredding of incriminating evidence, is not just a modern phenomenon. We find it in
the Bible as well, sometimes with the most illustrious
of personalities.

See Aaron's response when his brother Moses con-
fronted him about the heinous sin of the golden calf:

> And Moses said to Aaron, What did this people unto
> thee that thou hast brought so great a sin upon them?
> And Aaron said, Let not the wrath of my lord glow,
> thou knowest the people that they are set in evil. For
> they said unto me, Make us gods which shall go
> before us: for this Moses, the man that brought us up
> out of the land of Egypt, we know not what is become
> of him. And I said unto them, Whosoever hath any
> gold let them pull it off. So they gave it to me, then I
> cast it into the fire, and there came out this calf.
> (Exodus 32:21–24)

Certainly not a forthright admission here. For all his
unassuming nature, Aaron could not bring himself to say,
"I have sinned."

And what of Saul, the first king of Israel? In the battle
with Amalek, Saul had let live Agog, the king of Amalek, as
well as their cattle, in contravention of the explicit instructions of the prophet Samuel (1 Samuel, chapter 15).
Note Saul's response to Samuel's rebuke:

And Samuel came to Saul and Saul said unto him: Blessed be thou of the Lord; I have performed the commandments of the Lord. And Samuel said: What is the bleating of the sheep in my ears and lowing of the oxen which I hear? And Saul said: They have brought them from the Amalekites; for the people spared the best of the sheep and of the oxen, to sacrifice unto the Lord thy God; and the rest we have utterly destroyed.

So Saul found it difficult (impossible?) to say simply "You're right. I did wrongly." It was, first of all, "the people who spared the oxen" and, furthermore, they did so for a worthy cause, "to sacrifice unto the Lord thy God!"

While Saul blamed the people and then weakly tried to justify their actions and Aaron blamed the people and ascribed the calf's creation to ill fate ("and there came out this calf"), the morally robust Judah blamed himself and exonerated Tamar.

Now compare this with Judah's grandson, David. How did he face an accusation of guilt?

After the incident with Bathsheba, the Prophet Nathan goes to David and says:

Thou art the (guilty) man! Thus saith the Lord God of Israel: I annointed thee King over Israel and I delivered thee out of the hand of Saul . . . wherefore hast thou despised the word of the Lord to do that which is evil in My sight? Uriah the Hittite thou hast smitten with the sword and his wife thou hast taken to be thy wife and him thou hast slain with the sword of the children of Ammon. . . . And

David said unto Nathan: I have sinned against the
Lord. (2 Samuel 12:7–13)

What a breath of fresh air! No hesitation, no fault-
finding, no blame-placing, no extenuating circumstances;
in short, no excuses. A straightforward admission of guilt.
Vis à vis Nathan, David was in the position of power. To
paraphrase Napoleon, "How many battalions did Nathan
have?"! David had no need to bow to Nathan. But this
was the grandson of Judah, a man above the crowd—a
man who takes responsibility before man and God, a king
in Israel.
Is this stretching a point? Open up the Book of Second
Kings, chapter 20. Start with verse 12 where we read
about Hezekiah, grandson of David, descendant of Judah,
King of Israel:

At that time Berodach-baladan, the son of Baladan,
king of Babylon, sent a letter and a present unto
Hezekiah for he had heard that Hezekiah had been
sick. And Hezekiah hearkened unto them and showed
them all his treasure-house, the silver, and the gold,
and the spices, and the precious oil, and the house of
his armor, and all that was found in his treasures;
there was nothing in his house nor in his dominion
that Hezekiah showed them not. Then came Isaiah
the prophet unto the king Hezekiah, and said unto
him: What said these men? and from whence came
they unto thee? And Hezekiah said: They come from
a far country, even from Babylon. And he said: What
have they seen in thy house? And Hezekiah answered:
All that is in my house have they seen; there is
nothing among my treasures that I have not shown

them. And Isaiah said unto Hezekiah, Hear the word of the Lord. Behold, the days come that all that is in thy house and that which thy fathers have laid up in store unto this day shall be carried to Babylon, nothing shall be left, saith the Lord. . . . Then said Hezekiah: Good is the word of the Lord which thou hast spoken. . . .

The prophet confronts the king with wrongdoing and foretells his punishment, the terrible defeat and pillage at the hands of Babylon. And Hezekiah, the Judah-ic, David-ic king of Israel, accepts the rebuke and the punishment with nary a whimper. His response—a stoic (or Judaic) "Good is the word of the Lord."

David and Hezekiah, both kings of Israel/Judah, all evince the same telltale personality trait of their fore-bearer, Judah. Unabashed forthrightness, personal integrity, the ability to accept responsibility for wrongdoing without rationalization, these are the qualities of the Messiah of Israel. The characteristic which was already apparent generations earlier in Judah's simple admission, "She is more righteous than I."

When we look again at that story of Judah and Tamar we see the awesome beauty of the moral. For only after Judah took full responsibility for his actions, then and only then could a Peretz be born. Certainly, had Judah let the pregnant Tamar burn, there could have been no Peretz.

. . . And Peretz begat Hezron; and Hezron begat Ram; and Ram begat Amminadab; and Amminadab begat Nahshon; and Nahshon begat Salmah; and Salmon

begat Boaz; and Boaz begat Obed; and Obed begat
Jesse; and Jesse begat David. (Ruth 4:18–22)

Interpretation in this case consists of no more than
perceiving the threads that bind together different parts
of the Scriptures. Those who see the Scriptures as fragments patched together, as parallel and/or contradictory
oral traditions, would be less attuned to such long-dis-
tance connections. The present interpretation assumes
an interconnectedness within the Scriptures. The above
analysis points out more than this, however. It points
up a psychological, moral, and historical connectedness
that goes beyond mere text analysis. Although we really
know very little about the biblical personalities, when
we view them as real, three-dimensional people we come
away with psychological insights that otherwise would
have escaped us. We expect to find stability in personality
traits in our day-to-day life; we have all reason to expect
this in biblical personalities. When, indeed, we do find
it, often in a most low-key expression, our respect for
the authenticity of the biblical record is reinforced. It
rings true.

14

One Last Key

At this point I can only hope that the reader has also been bitten by the fascination with the multifaceted splendor of the Torah-text. It is that fascination which has fueled my lifelong love for Torah study and which prompted me to write this book.

But before I close this beginning guide to Torah interpretation, I would like to add one more Key. You will recall the provocative gentile who asked Hillel for the essence of the Torah while standing on one foot. Hillel's famous answer concluded with an open invitation, "The rest is interpretation. Go and learn." It was our jumping-off point for a discussion on interpretation, but without the gentile's question Hillel never would have been prompted to give his classic answer. Without the question nothing happens; without questions The Book remains a closed book no matter how often we open it.

Asking the cogent, focused question is the yin of interpretation; answering the question is the yang. When sitting down to read the Torah, an attitude of puzzlement is essential. Nothing is to be taken for granted. It is with questions that we pry open the Torah's secrets; puzzlements are the oxygen that sustains us as we plumb its depths. Learning how to ask good questions is the starting point of every in-depth study.

Good questions have certain characteristics. They spring from the textual material itself, not from assumptions about the text. They are simple and straightforward, not convoluted. And once they are asked, they cannot be ignored. They disturb.

But not all questions need be answered. Good questions have a legitimacy of their own. They add to our understanding even before we can come up with an answer—and sometimes we glean insights precisely because we can't supply an answer. In such cases the significance of the knotty question derives not from cutting the knot but instead from the annoying fact that no analytic knife seems adequate to the task.

As an example of this, let's look at one of the most puzzling passages in the Torah. I refer to the story of Moses when he brought forth water from the rock (Numbers 20: 7–13). He took his staff, smote the rock, and quenched the thirst of the people. His behavior seemed to fulfill God's instructions. Yet immediately after his successful mission we read: "And the Lord spoke to Moses and Aaron, Because you believed Me not, to sanctify Me in the eyes of the children of Israel, therefore you shall not bring this assembly into the land which I have given them" (Numbers 20:12). Moses and Aaron are severely punished. For what? The harsh Divine rebuke is totally unexpected and inexplicable.

The classical commentators struggled with this problem and have offered no less than thirteen different explanations as to what exactly Moses did that earned him the wrath of God and the painful punishment of being denied the right to enter the Land of Canaan. Everyone gets into the fray—Rashi, Ibn Ezra, Ramban, Rambam, the Ibn Atar, Eliezer Askenazi, Isaac Arama, the philosopher Yosef Albo, and others, all noted biblical commentators. Each decries and destroys previous interpretations as a preface to offering his own solution.

Looking over this commentators' battlefield, where interpretive casualties abound and with no undisputed conquerer in sight, one is left with the inescapable impression that this puzzle was meant to be. The text seems to be written in such a way as to withstand all attempts at deciphering it. Could it be that the Torah's ambiguity is intentional?

Why would that be? What purpose could that possibly serve? I would suggest that, in fact, the ambiguity of the text is no accident. The sudden and unexpected rebuke leaves us only with the knowledge that Moses sinned, yet without enabling us to know what his sin actually was. May it not be that it is precisely this ambiguity which makes the point the Torah wishes to convey?

Moses is the only man who stood at Sinai between the people and the Lord, who received the Tablets of the Covenant from the Almighty, the man about whom it was said, "And there arose not a prophet in Israel like Moses, whom the Lord knew face to face" (Deuteronomy 34:10). This man stood between the Divine and the human. The Bible has always made a point of the frailties of its great men, lest they be deified by the people. Moses was no exception. He too was fallible. But he was nevertheless unique, and the Torah preserves his uniqueness in precisely this way: that while we know he was fallible, we can never be privy to his particular weakness.

This interpretation finds its parallel in the way the Torah describes Moses' death, that great equalizer, that which even the Man of God could not escape:

> So Moses, the servant of the Lord, died there in the land of Moab, according to the word of the Lord. And He buried him in the glen in the land of Moab . . . *but no man knows of his grave to this day.* (Deuteronomy 34:5–6)

It is made abundantly clear that although Moses succumbed, nevertheless, no man can stand at his graveside and point to it saying, "Here lies Moses." As his mortality is proclaimed, perceptible evidence of it is withheld from the rest of us. Likewise, in our puzzling text, as Moses' sin is announced, the precise nature of his sin is withheld. All this is accomplished by artful ambiguity. As students of the Bible we only become aware of the message by asking what must be asked and, after all our efforts, remaining puzzled.

Without questioning, the Bible remains a closed book. The inquisitive mind plunges beneath the text's shimmering surface, descending into a colorful, vibrant world of never-ending pleasures of the mind and soul. Asking questions is our Master Key to understanding.

15

A Final Word

I can't end this book without making explicit what has been implicit throughout my discussion of Torah interpretation: The study of Torah is a joyous experience! Serious, rigorous work, but a joy all the same. Challenging, rewarding, inspiring, and joyous.

And at the risk of sounding frivolous regarding the sacred Bible, I would say, It is fun. In defense, I would defer to David, king of Israel. His many panegyrics of the Torah include the following: "Were it not for your Torah, my plaything . . ." (Psalms 119:92) and "Thy Torah delighted me."

For generations *Cheder* children began their Torah studies with the Yiddish ditty "*Oilum HaBah iz a gutte zach. Lernen Toirah is a bessereh zach.*" Translation: "The World to Come is a good thing; learning Torah is even better!" Even the ultimate reward, the World to Come, is reduced to second place in the face of the Torah experience.

The Rabbis were so confident of the persuasive power of Torah study that they made the following startling midrashic interpretation of a verse in Jeremiah 16:11:

"Because your fathers have forsaken Me, says the Lord, and have walked after other gods, and have served them; *forsaken Me and not kept My Torah.*" Said Rav Huna and Rav Yirmiya in the name of Rav Hiya, the son of Abba [It is as if the Lord has said:] "Oh, that they would even forsake Me, as long as they keep studying My Torah, because when they are engaged in its study the light in it would lead them back to Me."

In the Jewish scheme of things, the spiritual rewards of the Afterlife and even the importance of the belief in God Himself take back seats to the centrality and significance of the study of Torah. This theme, implanted deeply in the Jewish mind over the millennia, would not have survived so vigorously had not the study itself been so satisfying an experience, so joyous an event.

When I read the Torah's words, I can't escape the awareness that I am reading words that have been read by millions before me. When I attempt to understand its messages, I am struggling with a challenge that has provoked myriads before me; I am engaged with mankind's oldest living legacy. If timelessness is a defining quality of Truth, then when I grapple with the meaning of a biblical story, poem, or law I am in touch with the closest thing on earth to immortal Truth. When I force the text to speak to me, cajole it into giving up its secrets, wrest from it an insight, I have had an encounter with the Eternal . . . and won! An experience of unequalled joy.

My final word—Open up the Bible, let your mind embrace it, and *enjoy.*

Index

About the Author

Avigdor Bonchek has a doctorate in clinical psychology from New York University and rabbinic ordination from Ner Israel Rabbinical College of Baltimore. He is a practicing psychotherapist who specializes in the treatment of anxiety disorders. He has been a lecturer at the Hebrew University of Jerusalem for the past twenty-five years. Previously he taught psychology at The City University of New York, Yeshiva University, and Ben Gurion University in Israel. Dr. Bonchek has taught Torah studies at The Ohr Somayach Center for Judaic Studies in Jerusalem and lectures extensively on both psychological issues and Torah topics. His book *The Problem Student: A Cognitive/Behavioral Approach* was published in Hebrew. He is presently working on two books, *Studying Rashi In-Depth,* in English, and *A Cognitive/Behavioral Psychology Reader,* in Hebrew. Dr. Bonchek lives in Jerusalem with his wife, Shulamit, and their six children.